Birds, Bats, and Baling Wire

Birds, Bats, and Baling Wire

by Kathleen Tresham Anderson

To Judy Fitzpatrick and Susan Wyatt who helped bring my vision into words and story.

To my husband, Tom, who let me follow my dream and came along with good grace as a fellow traveler.

ISBN 978-0-557-06178-5

Contents

Chapter One

IF DREAMS THERE BE

The road was ice-packed and the clouds, dirty white against the gray, closed in around us. The snowdrifts, piled up along the sides of the pavement, got wider and higher as we drove.

Beside the bank of a fast flowing river the road narrowed to a single lane and followed the river's curve. At one bend, the river was lost from sight. Tom and I drove a little further and stopped off to the side of a deserted country store. The snow was higher than the top of the van's windows. We got out, crossed the road, climbed over the top of the bank, and jumped into three feet of snow on the other side. In front of me was a small, dark red cabin with a path cleared to the door. Tom knocked. Janet Evans, the owner, opened the door and greeted Tom like a son she hadn't seen in ages.

Inside it was dark except for patches of light from windows in two of the wooden walls. The drifts of snow outside the windows seemed like a mountain range seen from a distance. Wooden furniture, large soft pillows and a fire in the woodstove created a cozy atmosphere. We sat down at a sturdy kitchen table and made do with a small gas lamp; there was no electricity in Goose Prairie.

The three of us spent a pleasant hour, Janet and Tom catching up on prairie happenings, while I learned a little about the folks of the Prairie. I heard unfamiliar names, but the inflection of their voices, the facial expressions at the mention of a name and the silence following the naming of another told me something about each person. They discussed the sick, the angry and difficult, those visiting over the winter and the ones who might sell come spring.

This was my first trip to Goose Prairie, Washington with Tom, my husband-to-be, whose Boy Scout Council camp was located there. The warmth of the fire, delightful conversation shared over good strong coffee, and abundant snow piled high outside gave me my first impression of winter at the prairie and a glimpse of life there in the darkest of seasons.

Each spring after we were married Tom and I spent weekends at Goose Prairie. The snow of winter left little piles of white fluff under trees. The sun was high in the sky and hundreds of daffodils pushed through to full bloom. People returned to the prairie, opened their cabins, hiked at the lower elevations, and enjoyed the mountains' beauty, all signaling a fresh start to a new year.

We practically lived at the prairie during the summers, Tom helping out at the camp and me enjoying the mountains. The trails were clear. Visitors camped in the woods, rode horses along the river trails, and trekked on the high peaks. The Goose Prairie Inn, a small café and general store, was open. Friends and strangers exchanged pleasantries, gossip, and mountaineering information over good, hearty food. The few permanent residents of Goose Prairie renewed friendships with cabin owners up for the summer months.

Weekend visits in the fall brought an eyeful of gold and red mixed with fading greens and blues. A touch of white high on the ridge from an early dusting of snow in late September was breathtaking. The animals' fast-paced activity, and the frosty mountain air brought nothing to my mind save the beauty of nature's changing landscape. I was a novice reader of the signs of nature in any season. Life in Yakima, down in the valley, was unaffected by these seasonal reminders so I had paid little attention to their meaning

My time at Goose Prairie was limited, but I loved the place and wanted to live there year around. It seemed a perfect location to realize a long-held dream. As a minister in the Presbyterian Church, I wanted to own and operate a retreat center that would be small, intimate, and aesthetically pleasing. It had to be affordable and in a reasonable location so Tom could continue his work with the Boy Scout Council in Yakima while I ran the retreat.

The first stories I heard about the Double K Mountain Ranch were told at the Goose Prairie Inn. Amid the closeness of stools and a mingling smell of coffee and bacon, Double K rumors passed from one person to another in hushed tones. Savory comments in return were greeted by whooping laughter or open-mouthed astonishment, decorum forgotten in the moment. It was said the ladies who owned the ranch rolled their own cigarettes, wrote many letters of complaint to Justice William O. Douglas about neighbors and the Boy Scout camp, and threatened visitors to the forest surrounding the Double K. And it was whispered the two women, Kay and Isabelle, had appointed themselves guardians of the wilderness and wanted to run it by their rules.

There were stories about those who stayed at the Double K – a governor's wife exercising between two Supreme Court Justices in the living room before breakfast, the executives of General Electric (from Pittsburgh, Pennsylvania) traveling on horseback into the wilderness, and guests being sent home when they didn't want to participate in planned activities. Tales were told of Justice William O. Douglas himself spending more time at the Double K than in his cabin next door.

It was reported that Isabelle did the cooking and fixed peanut butter and Walla Walla Sweets (an onion) for guests' lunches every day. She made carrot cake that was so good, people begged for more, and, to prepare meat for the evening meal, used pickling spices as a marinade. No extra helpings were allowed, and if people were late for breakfast or dinner, they were met with an empty plate or a good tongue-lashing.

Along with rumors and stories came the warning not to venture up the dusty dirt lane. One of the women had been known to threaten trespassers with a gun and the loss of their kneecaps. Rumors surfaced, then faded, and the ranch called the "Double K" took on a mysterious air. I began to look for a sign along the road pointing me toward this place. It had grown to mythical proportions in my mind.

And one day there it was: a dilapidated, rotting sign marking the lane as the entrance to the "Double K." A round circle of wood was split on one side and hanging by chains from two wooden poles, which were rotted and weather-beaten. The sign was amber red and needed paint. Leaning precariously looking like a strong wind would soon topple it, the round piece of wood was hard to separate from the young trees, bushes and weeds that surrounded it.

Every time I walked the dog or drove into Goose Prairie, I gazed at the sign and imagined what life would be like living there. I ventured a short way down the lane and hoped to see something that would give me clues to the mystery of the Double K. It was a game of "what if" played by my imagination and me.

During the summer of 1989 at a camp work weekend, Richard Cecil, the caretaker, mentioned the women of the Double K wanted to sell their place. They were in the process of meeting with prospective buyers. I approached Tom with the idea of buying it. His only question was "does it have city water and city sewers?" Taking this as a positive and affirmative response, I told Richard I wanted to meet the two women and tour the ranch. The thought of living in Goose Prairie and at the Double K was exhilarating. Richard made the arrangements and gave me a warning – *be on time!*

At the appointed hour late one summer evening a few days later, I drove up the lane I had passed for six years. A canopy of branches and leaves, created a myriad of green hues and shades of orange and red. Wildflowers bloomed alongside the drive. The holes, bumps, and curves in the lane, along with the musical sounds of the birds in the trees, contributed to the aura of my Double K dream. A field opened off the archway of trees and a beautiful flat piece of land with an old, but sturdy-looking wood beam barn, sat at one end. Remnants of post fencing dotted the fringe of trees surrounding the field. I followed the wandering lane up a small hill and as the car rounded a curve, I saw a tiny crooked cottage tucked into the forest on the right. To the left sat a larger cabin covered with moss and, in front of me stood a tall, long wooden structure.

The main ranch building was not what I had imagined. It was stark and out of proportion like a teenager caught in a growing spurt. Parking the car under the pines, I turned off the engine and sat in silence. The setting, the weather, the fading light through the trees, all enhanced the atmosphere. I got out of the car and walked along the gravel drive.

On my right, the lodge building's large paned windows allowed a view into what appeared to be the living room. It was huge. A few lamps were lit and a woman sat in a chair reading a magazine. I walked up to the back stoop, knocked on the screen door, and waited for someone to answer. The humming sound of a motor drifted up the hill as I waited. I knocked again. In a few seconds the door opened and a woman in her late seventies showed me in. She told me to be seated on a chair just inside the door and then left the room. I looked around quickly. My hands played with my shirttails, and my nervous leg bounced up and down as my heart tried to pound its way out of my chest.

The woman who had greeted me returned with another woman. This person was shorter, but sported the same type of outfit as the first – jeans, western shirt, kerchief tied around her neck, and old scuffed cowboy boots on her feet. Their walk as they came into the room was assertive and sure and they looked like they had just come from chewing tobacco or swinging a rope over a calf. The shorter woman sat down opposite me while the taller one stood. They introduced themselves. The woman who had met me at the door was Isabelle and her partner was Kay.

There was no small talk. Kay seemed to be the boss and shot the first question at me.

"What makes you think you could run a place like this?"

I thought for a moment – what *did* make me think I could run a place like this?

"I worked on a little island off the west coast of Scotland. I cooked for a hundred people a day and bought all the food from the mainland for delivery. It was a guest retreat center and I was involved in all aspects of its operation. Also, I worked in a motel once as a maid – I can make hospital corners."

No change in their facial expression. They stared at me and I began to ramble.

"I have stayed at retreat houses. I worked in restaurants during college. I've gone to seminary and been a minister for eight years. I know how to relate to all kinds of people. My husband is capable of doing most anything, including major plumbing repair. He's very handy and has lots of tools we could bring with us."

I couldn't judge whether this was going well. After a few more questions from them and my feeble offering of answers, the interview was over.

Kay had the final word. "Okay, we'll be in touch."

I left the kitchen of the lodge trying to appear calm, but light-headedness and a peculiar floating feeling in my body, were signs of a different emotion. Elation – unsupported elation. I knew nothing more than I had before I parked the car except that the Double K should be mine.

Back at camp, Tom, ever the practical, logical, grounding presence in our relationship, was not elated when I shared "the interview" story. *How much? What about the sewer system? Are they on city water? (A joke) What about Katy and school next year? Does the school bus come all the way up to the prairie?*

Granted, those were all excellent questions, but I didn't want to hear them. I gave Tom a quick synopsis. The women had not talked price and they did not give me a tour (except in the area closest to the back door). They did not answer any of my questions because I was too intimidated to ask them. For Tom, this lack of information added to the absurdity of purchasing the Double K. It was an inconsequential hurdle to me.

With autumn approaching, and our family making fewer trips to the prairie, the question of purchasing the Double K was shelved. Tom thought I might forget about it and by the time spring rolled around again, the place would be sold and unavailable. He hadn't considered the recesses of my mind where dreams flourished: The Double K rooms filled with down comforters, pillows abounding; and scrumptious meals of gourmet foods served in the dining room. Guests, lounging in the comfort of the great room beside a roaring fire, would warm their outsides while an after-dinner aperitif would intensify the enjoyment on their insides. I had sensed the aura and ambiance of the place from sitting in that kitchen for fifteen minutes. That was enough for my dreams to take hold and root.

We returned to Goose Prairie in late spring of the following year. Tom was getting the camp ready for summer activities and I hung out at the Goose Prairie Inn. It was the best place to hear news about local events. Gossip! I didn't know people from the prairie very well, but I liked to hear the news even if I weren't a contributor.

I sat at the counter with a cup of coffee and listened to the conversation around me. A person two stools down talked about the most newsworthy gossip of all. A couple from Seattle had purchased the Double K. The sale was final and they would be moving to the ranch in August.

For a moment I couldn't breathe. My coffee cup hung suspended in midair. I briskly tried to wipe away the tears spilling onto my cheeks. The bottom had dropped out of my fantasy world.

Sadness overwhelmed me when I passed the Double K sign at the end of the lane each day. Considering I'd never really seen anything but the kitchen sink, a corner of the dining room, and the back door lit by the late summer sun fading over the crest of the hill, it was a silly kind of sadness. What was so odd was at the same time, I still felt I was the rightful owner. I did know the place intuitively, despite my lack of physical knowledge of it. What seed had been planted and how long would it be before it pushed its way into the sunlight?

Chapter Two

A SECOND CHANCE

On the Friday before the Fourth of July, Richard came into the Goose Prairie Inn and said Kay and Isabelle wanted to see me. I was shocked. How had they remembered my name let alone that I was at the camp? Richard seemed hesitant to tell me the news.

"The sale with the Seattle people fell through. Kay and Isabelle purchased a house in Yakima and want to be out of the lodge by August. They don't want to spend another winter here."

A second chance! I thought about this for a while. The women at the Double K were flirting with me as a buyer. I could reconsider the nature of a desire and dream that had no foundation or I could run with it.

I welcomed this potential conversation as Don Quixote welcomed his Dulcinea. That evening I went to my second interview. This time, I was someone important. We greeted each other warmly. I got to sit in the living room and we *did* chitchat. They invited Tom and me to have a tour of the buildings, barns and land the next day.

Dancing all the way back to the camp, I related the news to Tom. Although he was willing to go see the Double K, he agreed only to give it an hour. He had work to do at the camp. He wasn't going to show enthusiasm for my reckless dreaming.

My mind was racing, my heart pounding, and my imagination running wild when I went to bed that night. I was entranced by the dream of ranch ownership. I envisioned famous people knocking on the door, write-ups in the newspaper, and television programs featuring life at the Double K Ranch. I wanted to laugh out loud, sing phrases of songs, and jump on the mattress. But every so often a wave of nervousness and fear washed over the joy and I woke the next day exhausted but excited.

The weather was sunny and cool, the sky a brilliant blue hue with a few wisps of white clouds floating slowly like feathers in a soft breeze. The shadows of the trees with the forest windows of bright sunlight created the perfect mood as we drove up the lane. The field in front of the lodge was basking in full summer sun, and the barn sat in an even more picturesque position than I remembered. We were driving into my dream. From the look on Tom's face, one would have thought we were driving into a nightmare.

Chapter Three

HOW COULD ANYTHING BE SO PERFECT?

K ay and Isabelle greeted us at the back door. They were extra friendly towards Tom and warmed to him immediately, which surprised me because they had made it quite clear over many years, through letters to Justice William O. Douglas, that they had no use for the Scouts or their camp a mile up the road. Now they were anxious to show us around the place. We began in the basement.

It was dark and dusty so we used flashlights to illuminate the stops on this part of the tour. Patches of light from three coal-dust covered windows made stepping stone outlines on the dirt floor. Our first stop was the coal furnace, a huge black square with a small door for wood and coal. Kay assured us that when it was operating in the winter it heated the whole house, even the second floor. Isabelle talked about pipes, cleaning the system, and how we could save money by being our own chimney sweeps. Their fingers pointed here and there as they offered vague explanations of water heater operations, coal delivery systems, and summer ventilation. I wasn't very interested in these topics but I saw that Tom was intrigued by the women's unusual methods and the mechanics of the ranch's operation.

Along one basement wall was a water heater and right next to that a wringer washer. It looked exactly like one I had seen in a 1920's ad for laundry power.

"Do you use this?" I thought they had just been too lazy to move it out, but Isabelle's raised eyebrows and look of disgust shot that statement in mid-air.

"Of course. You can't have a washing machine up here. It uses too much electricity and is far too expensive. This machine is the best wringer made and it does a good job. That's all *we* ever needed." Whoa! A reminder that I was the city girl and would have to rid myself of the frivolous idea of a washing machine.

"Where do you dry the clothes?" There were clotheslines strung around the basement, but surely with all the coal dust and dirt they wouldn't dry clean clothes down here.

"In summer we hang them outside, but in winter we just hang them from these lines and eventually they dry. The heat from the furnace helps."

"Do you dry the sheets down here as well?"

"Of course. Where else would we hang them?" The sharp, impatient answer carried with it the implication that my questions were inane. White sheets and black coal didn't seem like a good combination to me, but if that's what they did, I could do that as well. They had used this system for forty years. Who was I to question their procedure?

We walked behind the staircase into the other half of the basement. A huge old door strung with wire running from each corner to the ceiling above, hung in the middle of room.

"What's that for?" I asked. A few vegetables were lying in the middle of the door.

"We rigged that to keep rodents and other small animals away from our fruits and vegetables. This way they can't get to them from the floor." Rodents? Other small animals? There were two heavy wooden cellar doors standing open to the back of the property and the forest beyond. Why didn't they just close the doors?

So many questions, but I didn't want to ask them all at once in case they thought I wasn't smart enough to run the Double K. Bringing a notebook to write them down would have been a good item to have, but it was too late now.

Kay pointed out a refrigerator in the corner of the basement. It was an old Dometic brand, gas-operated refrigerator similar to those found in an RV. It was standing on a sturdy, wooden crate.

"We keep the temperature setting very low so that it acts as a freezer. It has worked well for years." These women might look like cowboys, but they were clever as housewives making due on a small budget. We'll just stick to their plan until something better comes along, I thought.

We climbed the basement stairs into the kitchen, getting a quick lecture on the big black woodstove tucked against the back wall. We looked at the three poorly painted metal sinks, received instructions on how to paint them with marine grade paint, and headed up the next flight of stairs.

The bathrooms were first on the second floor tour. Each one had a toilet in a stall, one sink, and a metal shower. The shower was painted the same ghastly marine greenish blue as the sinks in the kitchen. There were also pipe fittings for another sink and a stall and hole in the floor for another toilet.

"Why weren't more sinks and toilets installed? " Tom asked. "The fittings are all there."

Kay answered this time. "After we built the place we realized that only one person at a time was going to use the bathroom so why bother adding the extra fixtures. And over the years no one's ever needed to use the bathroom with someone else, so I guess our theory was correct."

How could they use it at the same time if the fixtures weren't there, I wondered, but I kept that particular thought to myself.

To the left of one bathroom was a large corner bedroom with a red-blanketed double bed and a forest view from two sets of windows. The walls and ceiling were light colored tongue-and-groove pine paneling. The floor was a darker pine but held the same natural wood beauty as the walls. In the corner was a small closet without doors and on top of it were lots of books held upright by two metal bookends. The beauty of the room was exquisite. I was stunned that these two women, so brash in their social habits, could create such a place. The simplicity of the décor, the natural wood and diffused sunlight, radiated peacefulness and calm. It was the perfect place for solitary meditation and the experience of nature's healing touch. There was seamlessness between the room and the forest outside its windows. How could anything be so perfect?

We walked down the short hallway with its double room and two tiny singles and turned past the stairs. The other hall was lined with six twin-bedded rooms, three rooms on each side. Each room was decorated in this simple way: white linens, a pillow, and a thick red woolen blanket used as a spread on each bed. A grey blanket of similar fabric was folded neatly and lay on the foot of the mattress. Books in neat rows sat on top of the closets in the rooms and all the rooms had windows looking out over the forest. I loved it!

I glanced at Tom who was looking behind the doors, out the windows, and sitting on the beds to test the mattresses. He was getting excited and I could tell he was beginning to see the potential of this property.

Our next stop on the tour was the attic where we saw the chimney and its flue.

"This flue," Isabelle said, "is important to the operation of the woodstove in the summer. Just take off this cover and put a lit piece of paper in there. The stove will light then." Whatever. I wasn't interested in a hole in the chimney, not with all this beautiful wood surrounding me.

The attic was composed of two large spaces divided by the grand, stone chimney. The floor was unfinished pine tongue-

and-groove planking and the roof was steeply pitched, giving the room a cathedral-like appearance. The vastness of the empty space set my thoughts in motion, racing from one corner of my mind to another, imagining what we could do with it.

"Do you want to see the generators and the pump house?" A voice broke into my brain's meanderings. I was all set to say no, but Tom gave a definitive yes. He was totally engrossed in the place and that scared me a little. I depended on him to be the voice of reason. What if we both became dreamers? Who would be left to tug on the reality chain?

Outside we headed downhill to the generators that were housed in a garage-type building without doors. Looking inside, I was reminded of a junk store. Ropes and chains of all sizes hung from the side walls and one, five, and fifty-gallon drums stood on the dirt floor underneath. The backseat of an old World War One military supply truck took up one corner and a large tire from a deuce-and-a-half army truck leaned against it. A small door on the back wall was open to another room that housed the two generators, one a fairly new diesel model and the other a twenty-year-old gasoline-powered type. Screwdrivers, hammers, and wrenches lay scattered around on the oil and gasoline splattered dirt floor and, in one section of the tiny room, number ten cans were lined up like tin soldiers at-ease waiting to be dismissed. Each one was filled with a mixture of washers, screws, bolts, nails, nuts and small pieces of odd-shaped metal fittings. Nothing was sorted according to size or dimension, but thrown together like clean-out-the-refrigerator vegetable soup. I looked at Tom and his face shone with delight at the sight.

His grandfather had owned a lumberyard and his father had been a partner in a hardware store. Materials of this kind, and in such quantity, excited him. There were so many cans with such a variety of hardware that if they became his he would have a sorting project for years to come. These treasure cans, I thought, will be enough to convince him to buy the ranch.

We left the garage (Tom reluctantly) and walked down the gently sloping back lane. The soft, powdery soil sent little puff-clouds of dust a few inches in the air with each step. The fir trees, some with diameters of three and four feet, stood like tall sentries at the wilderness boundary on the other side of the lane. Lankier trees, with their branches standing high on the trunk, reached out and up in search of sunlight in the wooded area to the right. A field with thick green grasses sat beyond the trees.

We approached the barn, a sturdy, two-story building, covered with the same gray, weathered shingles that covered the lodge and garage. A single aisle separated six cramped box stalls, three on each side. There was still hay in some of the hand-built wooden mangers on the sides of each stall. Holes, probably dug by impatient and space-deprived horses, dotted the hard ground inside the small space. Old, dried, leather halter pieces hung on the wall and were strewn on a mixture of straw and dirt covering one stall. It looked as if the horses had been turned out, never to return, and the barn left to nature's elements and the wild animals to arrange as they saw fit. Sunlight, filtered by cobwebs hanging thick around the window frames, created symmetrical patterns on the floor of the stalls. Walking out the other end of the barn into the full sunlight we found ourselves in the field we had spotted from the lane. Isabel and Kay stood in silence, looking across the field, and then, as if remembering that we were there, Isabelle spoke.

"We kept the horses here in the summer and left from this field on all of our pack trips up to Cougar Lake and beyond." Her voice sounded sad and wistful.

"Did you keep them here in the winter?" The barn was far too small for the herd of horses I imagined they needed to carry a group and supplies up into the mountains for a three-or-four day trip.

"No, we put them in pasture down the valley in Naches. The snow is far too deep in winter without adequate barn space for the horses to keep them here. But we haven't had horses in several years, at least for the guests." I knew from conversations with people on the Prairie that Kay had served in the Second World War in the Red Cross and that both women were in their late seventies, if not early eighties. No wonder the horses had been gone for a while.

We began walking across the field, smaller pines and firs circling the area with the larger trees providing the backdrop. Gopher holes punctuated the ground and the soil that was turned over was black and rich looking, like prepared potting soil from the store. A small concrete block building came into view as we approached the end of the field near the road. It was housing for the well's pump and pipes.

All of us couldn't fit inside at once. I elected to stay outside, hovering around, pretending interest by occasionally popping my head in the door. Tom was the handyman and all-around mechanical person and his interest was keen. I walked a few feet from the pump house, felt the cool breeze, took in the sunlight highlighting the open space and listened to the birds. Moving from tree to bush and back to the trees, they noisily reminded me that I was trespassing in their domain.

Kay, Isabelle and Tom emerged from the pump house. We walked slowly up the drive, Tom asking the questions, Kay and Isabelle notably delighted by his knowledge and experience with similar equipment. I silently breathed in all the beauty and sacredness of this place, a pristine, undisturbed haven from modernity. And yet, without intruding heavily on the forest, it had necessary conveniences like toilets, lighting, and heating. I was so taken with this short experience at the Double K, I couldn't figure out what questions to ask Kay and Isabelle or what comments to offer as proof of my competence to run the ranch. I did know that I had to have this place. Of that I was certain.

Our foursome had made a complete circle around the ranch and we now arrived at our vehicle parked in the gravel drive. Tom and I got into the car, thanked Kay and Isabelle, said we'd be in touch with them very shortly, and slowly drove down the lane. Neither of us uttered a word until we arrived at the Boy Scout camp a mile up the road. I stopped the car, turned off the ignition, and ventured into the arena of discussion first.

"What do you think?"

"I don't know what I think. It's a wonderful place but it needs lots of labor-intensive work done. The routine maintenance has been neglected and there's a lot of junk lying around. Barbed wire, wood, old car parts. All that kind of stuff. I don't know where we will get the money." I didn't have an answer to that question, but I felt relieved that he was excited and not negating the idea entirely.

Tom got out of the car and headed toward the dining hall. I picked up our five-year-old daughter Katy from the trading post where she was waiting with some of the camp staff who had taken care of her for the morning. I put her into the car seat and drove down the road, heading toward Yakima and home, an hour's drive from Goose Prairie. Katy fell asleep, which left me time to contemplate my dream and come up with a plan to make it happen.

At home, I waited for Tom to arrive from camp. The ultimate decision would be his, not because he was the boss but because his understanding of finance and actual expense was much greater than mine. In my mind, I was busy decorating, welcoming guests, going for walks with the dogs and soaking up the exquisite beauty of the forest surrounding the Double K. I knew that Tom was thinking about mortgage payments, interest rates, insurance, Katy's education, and what reasonable income we might expect from the ranch's patronage that would help pay for the ranch itself. At 2:20 p.m. that afternoon he came striding in the back door.

"I think we should go for it!" His excitement and confidence startled me, and I began asking the practical questions.

"Can we make enough for the mortgage payments? Will we have enough money to live on? How will we make a down payment? Where will we get financing?" These were the questions we worked to answer in the next few days and weeks.

Chapter Four

FRANKLY, MY DEAR,
THEY DON'T GIVE A DAMN

W here would we get financing? We had borrowed money for cars and our house, paid it back without incident, and had a great credit rating. So, I would approach the bank that we used for our personal banking. It was local and our family had been customers for six years.

Dressed in my classiest clothes, I emerged from the elevator on the ninth floor of the bank building. In the mirror across from the elevator, I checked my outfit and hair then signed in with the receptionist. She rang the loan officer who arrived in the reception area a few minutes later. My would-be benefactor was dressed in a black business suit, her dyed reddish-brown hair caught up in a French twist.

Greeting me with a warm smile and weak handshake, she led me down the hall to a conference room. Several chairs were neatly placed around a polished wooden table and a large picture window framed the blue sky outside. We sat close to the window where the view to the mountains was quite beautiful, but the area down at street level, with its run-down houses, car parts, and trash filled yards, told a different story.

I began the recitation of our plan to buy the ranch, what money we had to put down, and how we planned to add to our income through the ranch's guest business.

"It sounds wonderful. But the bank will not finance this project because there's no electricity."

"There is electricity," I said. "We have to generate it ourselves, that's all. And since we do it ourselves, it's probably more reliable than the electricity you're getting here in this building." I was trying to sound positive.

"Financial institutions will not finance properties without a utility like electricity coming from a certified source."

"You mean to say that the shack below us in that neighborhood has more chance of being financed than our gorgeous mountain property with a nine bedroom, six- thousand square foot lodge on it?" What little respect I had for bankers was ebbing like the tide at Coney Island.

"That is correct."

"So, what you're telling me is that the bank has one pat answer for everyone and there's no room for creative solutions?" I paused and took a deep breath trying to push aside my frustration. "There are other banks. I'll go to them."

Pushing around a pad of paper on the table, she looked at me, and then rose from her chair. I got up, grabbed my purse and stomped out, indignant that she and her bank were too rigid to consider our plan and act on it.

Yes, there *were* more banks and I visited most of them, but at each one the story was the same. Too much risk without enough amenities to justify taking that risk.

A close friend, who owned an orchard, suggested we make an appointment with another local bank whose primary business was loaning money to ranchers and farmers. Perhaps they would understand the rural life and the rewards found therein. Maybe they wouldn't care about the lack of public electricity.

Tom came with me to the bank this time. We checked in with the receptionist, took a seat and waited a few moments. The loan officer, whose name was Dick, came out of a small room across from where we were seated, shook Tom's hand, and led us into his office.

Dick pointed to several straight back chairs on one side of the desk, and dropped his hefty body into the cushioned executive chair. He picked up a pencil, held the eraser end in one hand and the point in the other, and pushed on the edge of his desk. The chair teetered backwards.

"Well, how can I help you folks?"

He asked questions and Tom and I took turns answering them. There were questions about our backgrounds, the history of the ranch, and the location of Goose Prairie. He also wanted to know about Kay and Isabelle. Odd, nosy questions for a banker to be asking but what could we do? We needed the money.

There was a brief pause in the conversation and I, feeling hopeful, asked what he thought about giving us a loan.

"Oh, we don't finance anything like this. Too risky. I could have told you that over the phone."

I took a deep breath, ready to launch into my lack of creativity in bankers speech when Tom, sensing my rising anger, politely excused us from Dick's office. He escorted me out the door and into the parking lot in front of the bank.

"What an idiot! What a pompous jerk!" I kicked off my shoes, lifted my dress, and yanked the panty hose down from my hips, over my calves and off my feet.

"I am never," I shouted toward the bank, "never going to put on panty hose for anyone again! Ever! Especially uncreative bankers who masquerade as human beings!"

I got in the car, shut the door and cried. I was frustrated at my inability to solve this problem, angry with institutional thinking about money, and painfully scared this was the end of the Double K for us.

Kay's nephew, Bob, was in contact with us about the purchase of the ranch on a regular basis. He wanted to get his aunt and Isabelle moved before winter made it impossible. Tom told him we still hadn't gotten a bank loan. He asked which banks we had approached, and, on hearing that we had pretty well exhausted our prospects, said he would get back to us.

A few days later, Tom came home from work early.

"Bob is willing to lend us the money to buy the ranch. He wants to go over the arrangements and believes his offer is fair to us, and, to him for the risk he's incurring in lending to us." At this point I was willing to sell my soul to finance this project.

The next day, we went to Gleed, a small rural area outside of Yakima, where Bob's office was located. I dressed nicely, but didn't jinx the meeting with hosiery. This meeting had several parallels with my banking experiences like the straight back chairs, the office, and the desk. I felt a little uneasy, but kept reminding myself that this time we would be getting the money. My hands were a bit shaky and my heart was beating faster than usual. Bob was our last chance for financial backing and if it didn't work out financially with him, we were done.

After a few minor formalities, Bob presented his plan. He was friendly, but appropriately business-like, enough to help me feel confident in his proposal. We would pay him a certain amount up front as a fee for borrowing the money then we would pay two percent over the prime interest rate on the monthly mortgage payments. At the end of five years, there would be a balloon payment. All of this seemed reasonable to me, but I had enough presence of mind to defer to Tom. From his face, I could see that he was quickly doing the math. I heard them talking about details, but I was creating a timeline in my mind for all of this to happen.

"Okay," I heard Tom say. "It sounds like it will work."

A few hours later, when we walked out of his office, all the arrangements concerning settlement and closing dates were done. I was ecstatic in a hesitant kind of way. There was no turning back.

With the bulk of the financing secure, we moved ahead with our other planning. At home we sorted through all of our household goods to be sold at a yard sale in a few weeks. We figured out what we needed and what things we didn't. Electrical appliances, except for the mixer and the coffee pot, were the first to go since we'd only be able to use them with the generator operating and economically that wasn't feasible. No more electric curling irons, electric rollers, popcorn makers or ice crushers. No more crock-pot, hand mixer, or electric can opener. The electric blankets and pencil sharpener were quickly tossed into the garage sale pile. The money we would make from the sale would be used as seed money to buy dishes, towels and other items for the guests at the ranch.

Our house, a lovely, old two-story with charm and character, went on sale. The market was strong and we knew we would get the asking price. We needed the money as a down payment on the ranch and we needed it soon. A buyer was secured within a week of listing. They were odd people with allergies who had come from the East and wanted wooden floors. We had them, so they made an offer.

We continued sorting through our household goods over the next few weeks. Several times I experienced bouts of bad pain across my midsection and between my shoulder blades. One Sunday in July, I could no longer pretend all was fine. I was incapacitated. Lying on the family room floor where it was cool I breathed shallowly like a woman in childbirth. I didn't eat and within twenty-four hours, the pain subsided. The next day, I had an important all day meeting at a restaurant in the mountains and drove for an hour. My lunch consisted of water and ice tea but the pain returned in waves, and, after a few hours, I excused myself. I called the doctor's office as soon as I returned to Yakima.

"How bad is the pain?" The receptionist asked.

"It's coming in waves and then going away for a short time."

"How long have you had it?"

"Since Sunday morning."

"I can schedule you to see the doctor next week on Tuesday at 2 p.m." A wave of nausea passed over me as I thought about waiting until the next week. But maybe the pain would subside before then and I wouldn't have to go at all.

The next day, I felt worse and called the doctor's office again.

"I really am sick now," I whined, "And I need to see the doctor today." There must have been a sense of urgency in my voice because I got an appointment an hour later.

I sat in the examining room on a table covered with white paper. When the doctor walked in, she gasped.

"We need to test you immediately! You are yellow, jaundiced. You may have hepatitis."

"Is that the only thing I could have?"

"No. Do you still have your gall bladder?" I wasn't sure where it was in my body, but I was pretty sure it was still there.

"Yes."

"Then you may be having gall bladder attacks. We'll see after the test."

I waited for the results and was relieved to hear that I did not have hepatitis, but the alternative wasn't great either. It was my gall bladder.

The next Monday, prepped for surgery, I was wheeled in to the operating room and relieved of the body part causing the problem. When I awoke, I was in a single room. Tom was there, as well as our real estate agent. The buyers for our house had made a final offer and it needed to be approved and signed. The agent made sure that I was coherent and passed me the papers. As I drifted back into restless sleep, it was comforting to know that the down payment for the ranch was secure. The pieces were falling into place nicely and we would soon be living at the Double K.

Chapter Five

POSESSION IS NINE-TENTHS OF THE LAW

Signing papers for possession of the ranch was anticlimactic after the anxiety of finding money to make it happen. Arrangements for the move went quickly. Our huge garage sale began one morning at six and most of the household goods were gone by eight. With the income from the sale we were able to hire a moving van, buy packing boxes, and begin purchasing necessities for the ranch guests, whoever they would be.

Tom and I decided we would add to our own dish set, expanding it to service for twenty-four. We went to the local Sears and bought towels, washcloths, and hand towels in a neutral color so they would be easy to replace. I loved all this shopping and choosing. It was like putting muscle and skin on the skeleton of my thoughts.

We began the tedious task of packing and labeling boxes, then piling them in the living room. There were stacks set aside for the ranch attic, basement, our small apartment, and the main lodge rooms. My books would be sorted out and added to the ones that sat on the top of the closets in each room. Since the storage space for clothing and other personal items was extremely limited in the apartment, we would put the majority of our clothing in the attic and exchange them each season.

The surgery limited my ability to help with lifting, bending, and anything else that taxed the incision. So I spent most of my time directing the packing, helping Katy organize her belongings, and sleeping. I had to get my strength back before our first guests arrived in September. Poor Tom. Every time we had moved I had been pregnant, sick, or on a business trip. And now, surgery. Maybe he was beginning to think that I was doing this to get out of helping.

Kay and Isabelle had a difficult time deciding on a day when they would move out. No one in their family was able to find time to get the ladies organized and moved. Tom and I arranged to help; otherwise we might never get to move in. We agreed Kay and Isabelle would take whatever they wanted from the ranch when they moved and what they left would be ours. Tom and a few of his friends, as well as a couple of Kay's younger relatives, packed the truck.

The women talked about the house in Yakima while packing.

"We have sprinklers but the system operates from the far south corner of the property. There's a well and we'll have to deal with that."

The property was outside of town and I assumed they had a few acres around the house. When we drove up to it I was shocked. The house was built of concrete brick. The front yard was small and a wall surrounded the tiny backyard with the sprinkler system. The south corner was just a few feet from the concrete patio.

Inside, the lounge chairs that had looked perfect in the little ranch apartment now looked worn and threadbare sitting in their linoleum-tiled living room. The furniture they had chosen to bring with them was old and tottery. Kay and Isabelle looked older and worn out in this environment as well. These women, who had lived at the Double K in the depths of the wilderness, been surrounded by wildlife, wooden floors, and seasonal forest changes, were now going to live in what I considered a concrete ghetto. How were they going to adjust to life in this linoleum floored, small windowed, utilitarian building?

As the truck pulled away from the house, the excitement of knowing that the Double K belonged to us was tinged with the sadness of leaving Kay and Isabelle there. The upside to this was that I was free to explore the Double K on my own and at my own speed. Tom and I didn't know exactly what we had bought, but we had a building, some land and the beginning of a new life.

My friend Maureen and I went to Goose Prairie to clean two days before the August 25 moving date. I was eager to look in the closets, browse among the books on the shelves, and see what the women had left in the apartment. When we arrived, a car was parked close to the lodge. I knew that the doors of the lodge weren't locked and for a few days, no one had been living there. I was concerned and wary.

As we came up to the back door, I heard voices and recognized them immediately. Kay and Isabelle!

"Hello," said Isabelle. "We've spent the last couple of nights here on the bed upstairs with our sleeping bags."

I'm sure I looked displeased.

"We've come to clean and rearrange things for the move on Saturday," I said.

Kay looked at me and smiled as she tied a rope around her sleeping bag.

"We're just packing up now. We'll be out of here as soon as we roll the sleeping bags."

My friend and I headed to the outside porch off the dining room. The paint on the stoop and the stairs was peeling and specks of it spotted the grass around the porch. Maureen lit a cigarette and laughed to herself.

"They're two gay old birds, aren't they now?"

"Where'd you get that idea?"

"Open your eyes, Kathleen." She laughed again. "They've been sleeping in that double bed up in the loft together for how many years?" She glanced at me and shook her head as she put out the cigarette in a glass ashtray on the corner of the porch. Before I could answer, footsteps sounded in the dining room. We got up, brushed ourselves off and went in.

"We're going now. We've got all our things. We wish you well."

As Kay spoke, I felt awkward and uncomfortable.

"Come visit when we get moved in. You're always welcome to visit us."

They smiled, said goodbye, and walked out the backdoor. I heard the car doors slam, the engine start and the crunching gravel become more and more faint. Maureen and I stood in silence for a few moments.

"Okay, enough mourning. Let's get busy!"

We did a fast cleaning of the kitchen, snooped in the drawers and cabinets, and looked on the shelves above the counter. There were two large crockery teapots which would hold enough tea for ten people. Odd strainers, food mashers, and other kitchen utensils filled the drawers. When we finished in the kitchen we went down to the apartment. It was 320 square feet with a small loft up above. The room had windows on two opposite sides and a fireplace on the wall between them. The rug covering a wooden floor was faded green and dirty. Along the other wall was the bathroom, which contained a small sink and a metal shower stall, painted the same marine green as the other sinks. Up above the living room and bathroom, the loft would provide our sleeping area. A narrow ladder staircase provided access to it. Katy would have one side of the loft for her bed and we would have the other.

The rest of the day was spent on light cleaning and commenting to each other on the treasures in the bedrooms and linen closet on the second floor. We peeked in the attic and the basement, but without electricity, it was hard to see what was in each place. Having satisfied my curiosity for the time being, I drove home, listening to suggestions for guest amenities from Maureen and coming up with ideas of my own.

Chapter Six

HELP WANTED

The truck arrived at the house in Yakima early Saturday morning and the moving men loaded it quickly. As soon as they finished, we locked the doors and headed to the mountains. At the Double K, a gentle, warm breeze rustled the leaves just enough to let us know it was there. Wispy clouds filtered the sun's light.

Many of our friends had assembled at the ranch. They sat on the front porch talking and laughing, waiting to help unpack and move some of the heavier items like the grand piano. Tom brought out a fresh pot of drip coffee every now and then, while we chomped on homemade cookies our friends had brought.

In less than two hours, we heard the sound of the heavy moving van coming slowly up the driveway, chains clanging at the bumps, the squealing sound of braking every few seconds. It stopped at the foot of the hill; the driver climbed out, and trudged up the driveway.

"Where's Tom Anderson?" Like magic, my husband appeared.

"I'm Tom. What seems to be the problem?" He walked toward the driver and the two of them walked back down the gravel lane, the driver gesturing towards the upper road. Tom returned shortly as the truck engine roared into action. Instead of coming forward, the truck backed up. Tom stopped at the porch landing.

"He says he can't make it up and around the driveway, so he's backing the truck up as far as he thinks is safe. He's going to Whistlin' Jack Lodge to call and tell his boss to send a smaller truck. He says they'll have to wait until the truck arrives before they can unload."

"That could be all afternoon," I said. "Why can't they just start with some of the smaller things and carry them up the driveway?"

"They don't do that. It's not in their contract."

This setback was annoying. The van service man had said there was no need for him to see the ranch driveway and lodge before the move. He was sure the truck would have no problem getting to it and unloading.

"I'll bring the camp truck over. We can unload from their truck and drive the camp truck to the house," suggested Richard, who was helping us with the move. "They can give us a hand with *that* can't they?"

The three moving men were sitting down by the little stream, smoking cigarettes, throwing rocks in the water, and playfully pushing each other around. Tom walked down to them and shared the plan. Since we were paying them by the hour and their salesman had sent the wrong size truck, I assumed that they would give us a hand with unloading the truck. They declined and said they had to wait for their own truck. So we all waited.

After several hours of wasted time, we asked them again. This time the movers agreed. They would help unload from the van and the rest of us would move the boxes and furniture into the house from the smaller camp truck. The volunteer crew would be hauling all our possessions up two flights of stairs to the attic, down one flight to the basement or all the way through the house and down three steps to the apartment. The people we'd hired would hand boxes to them and rest in between.

By the time the volunteer crew had moved most of our belongings to the lodge, the moving company's truck arrived. Finally, the people we were paying started earning their wages. They finished unloading the mattress, couches and chairs, and carried the large wardrobe boxes to the attic. Then they closed the doors of the van and were on their way.

Our friends sat down wherever they could find a space, on boxes, littered floors, and couches strewn with wrapping paper, to enjoy the bounty of food that they had brought with them as a celebration meal. One by one, they said their goodbyes, and we were left alone to unpack and begin our life at Goose Prairie.

The morning after the move, I was the first one up. Coming down from the loft in the apartment, I had the feeling that someone was watching me or was present in some form in the room. I put my robe on and walked up the first two steps of the three into the kitchen. Glancing out the window, which on the outside of the house was at ground level, I realized there were twelve eyes staring in at me.

Six raccoons were busily ripping into a fifty-pound bag of dog food we had left outside the kitchen's back door. They seemed to watch me without pausing from the task at hand. Their paws, each joint and bone clearly defined, looked like thin, miniature versions of the spooky hands displayed at Halloween. I was fascinated by the agile dexterity of those digits.

There were two large and four smaller raccoons. The larger ones were trying to keep the little ones away from the bag, but the little ones snuck around until they could get a paw in and gather handfuls of the tasty chunks of dog food. When each raccoon had a little pile, the group would become quiet and eat, always watching for movement toward the bag from the others. As soon as one moved, all the others began the routine again, big ones by the bag, little ones sneaking around getting what they could grab.

I was not sure of the proper etiquette for asking a group of raccoons to leave, so I opened the door, said a few little *shoo, shoos* and quickly shut the screen door in case they decided to attack. Finally after three such warnings, they lumbered a short distance away, but the largest raccoon stood on her back legs, turned quickly and came back, hissing at me the whole way, which emboldened the smaller ones. They, too, turned and, although keeping a much safer distance between them and me, they hissed as well. Stopping at various places on the driveway, eyeing me then the bag of dog food, me, and then the food again, they made a faint whining sound.

"Go on. Get." I was feeling more confident now that I knew they felt some fear. The hissing ceased for a few moments and then the biggest one started the sound again, but she moved no closer.

"Go on. Get out of here."

I came out the door, grabbed what was left of the dog food in the bag and shut the screen door as well as the wooden door. I wasn't taking any chances. We could share. They were welcomed to what was left on the ground and we had enough for a few days for our two dogs.

Chapter Seven

SCRUB-A-DUB-DUB

O ur first few weeks at the ranch were filled with jobs that had to be done before we could begin having paying guests. There were closets to clean out, linens to get organized, and pots and pans to inventory.

First, I tackled the mess in the second floor linen closet, a large pine-covered space with deep shelves from floor to ceiling and a big window opposite the door. The sheets, towels of varying sizes and condition, and extra red and white woolen blankets, were scattered about on the shelves like a rainbow gone astray. The blankets were heavy and when I lifted them off the shelf little black pellets fell into my hair and over my clothes. I threw the blankets down on the floor and madly brushed myself off.

On closer inspection, I realized the black dots were mouse droppings. There were lots of them. Carefully, I took the linens off the shelves one by one and shook them into the trashcan before laying them out on the hallway floor.

It was a disgusting job. When I finished removing most of them, I got the ladder and climbed up to look at the back of the top shelf. It was covered with droppings and pistachio shells. I removed tablecloths and napkins from the far back, swept each shelf, washed them down with a bleach solution, and lined the bottoms with paper. There were no holes where mice could sneak in and out. The only explanation was that the door to the closet had been left open too many times and the little vermin had become squatters.

No more, I thought. They can live in the basement and around the outside of the house, but not here. Not anymore.

Sitting on the floor outside the closet, I sorted through the various linens. The sheets were 100 percent cotton and in great shape, but the towels were threadbare and dotted with holes. There were fine cotton squares edged in lace, old-fashioned flowered tablecloths with matching napkins, and hand-crocheted doilies for the back and arms of upholstered furniture. Aprons of every size, shape and color, a few with fabric ties matching the apron material, others with simple white tie strings were piled together along with flour-sack dishcloths and fancier embroidered towels. Several beautiful pillowcases with tiny violets and wild flowers sewed across their borders lay among the plain cases. I was surprised by the delicate nature of these bed and table linens. In the little time I had spent with them, Kay and Isabelle never struck me as very dainty or feminine. They were women who had dared to live a life that few women would or could have chosen, fighting the harsh elements of snow, the lack of common conveniences, and the cultural bias against women running a ranch. I felt uneasy discovering this particular side of them in the linen closet. How long had it been since they'd used these beautiful things?

Everything needed to be washed and sterilized in the wringer washer in the basement. Starting with the sheets, I hauled them down the two flights, trying not to drag the white linens on the dirty basement stairs. At the bottom came the reckoning. How would I operate the wringer washer?

I shoved a few sheets into the top of the machine's cylinder. Attaching the hose to the laundry tub faucet, I began filling the washer with hot water and poured in some detergent. Within seconds, the water turned a nasty shade of brown-gray and the sheets, which had seemed white, were now light brown. I let them soak for a few minutes and drained the water from the machine. Filling it again with clean water and soap, I ran upstairs, switched on the small generator, and went back down to the basement.

Pushing the plug into the socket, I flipped a switch on the machine's side and it sprang to life. The agitator swooshed the sheets around in the tub while water lapped over the sides and covered the basement floor. The suds rose and fell like ocean waves. I watched in amazement as the washing machine danced its own rock and roll number near the sink. American Bandstand, next stop.

I pushed the switch down and the machine gradually became silent and still. With the hosepipe over the edge of the sink, I opened the washer's drain and let it empty. Filling the washer with clean water two or three times, agitating the laundry, and draining the filthy water, took up the afternoon.

After several hours, I had all the sheets, soaking wet, sitting in the laundry sink. Now I had to use the wringer. How was I going to turn the handle and put the wet sheets, each now weighing approximately a ton, through the small slit between the two pieces of the wringer?

I emptied the water out of the washer's cylinder, and put the sheets in it. Taking one corner of the piece of linen, I shoved it up to the slot and pushed it part way through the wringer to get it started. The first few times I turned the handle in the wrong direction and the sheet came tumbling out the way it had gone in. Finally, I remembered to turn the handle in the right direction and the sheet began releasing water back into the tub. All I could think of was "Rub-a-dub-dub, three men in a tub." Three men in *that* tub would have made the job much easier.

What I hadn't thought of was where the sheet would land after it went through the wringer. I stood beside the machine, one half of the sheet wrung and the other still in the tub. If I continued to wring it out it would be too big and heavy to handle without the possibility of dropping it on the coal-dust covered floor. I needed another laundry sink or a basket of some sort. The baskets were upstairs. Moving the handle backwards once again, I dropped the sheet back into the machine, ran upstairs, got the laundry baskets, and went back down to once again begin the process.

I hung them on the clothesline outside the basement door. It felt good to be in fresh air after spending time with mouse droppings and dirty laundry. But if I had to continue doing laundry this way when we had guests, I would be worn out before I reached my next birthday, which was only four months away.

I did laundry in this manner for the next two weeks and finally called it quits. We had to get a "real" washer and dryer and I didn't care how much electricity it took or that Kay and Isabelle had never used one at the ranch. I was willing to swallow my pride.

My time in the basement became almost enjoyable after the purchase of new appliances. The purr of the electric washer and the hum of the dryer were music to my ears, although I must admit I did miss the rock and roll entertainment of the old machine.

Chapter Eight

UNFORESEEN VISITORS

K aty stood on the porch in a new outfit, ready for her first-day-of-school picture, a tradition we started when she began pre-school. She was nervous about starting at a new school for first grade without the friends she had made in kindergarten, but she knew her new teacher and had been to school to see the classroom. She held Samantha, the dog, by her collar. Sam was willing to submit to this momentary diversion from the work of chasing squirrels, rabbits and birds, but her steep lean to the side away from Katy said she was ready to be released soon.

I was taking Katy to school and then continuing on to Yakima to my work at the church. I still had about four months until my contract was finished. Several hours twice a week, I visited members of the congregation, prepared my sermon and the service, and on Sunday, led worship and taught adult Sunday school. Since we didn't have many guests and the congregation was willing to be flexible about my schedule, I worked around what I had to accomplish at the Double K. It also meant several days a week the lodge was empty except for Sammy.

After school, I picked up Katy and we drove home. She slept most of the way, exhausted from getting up so early and the rigors of a full-day first grade schedule. Going from town into the mountains, where developments gave way to clumps of houses, then to homes dotting the roadway, and finally to remote cabins, slowed my mind and relaxed my body.

I pulled into the drive and parked beside the house. Immediately I had the feeling someone had been to the house. Being from the city, this alarmed me somewhat, but I dismissed it as a silly premonition. I woke Katy, grabbed some groceries from the back of the car and walked to the back door. It was ajar.

"Wait out here a minute, sweetheart."

"Why, mommy?"

"Because I want you to. I'll call Sammy and she can stay with you for a minute."

I poked my head around the door and there was Samantha, standing just a few feet away, wagging her tail expectantly. She came to the door and I let her out.

"Stay here with Sammy 'til I call you, okay, Katy?"

"Okay, but I'm hungry and I want a snack."

"I'll bring you a snack in a minute."

I went into the kitchen and looked around. Items on the counter had been moved. In the dining room, a piece of paper with a note scribbled on it lay on the table closest to the living room. Maybe one of the neighbors inviting us to dinner, I thought, feeling relief that it appeared no one was going to pop out and grab me. I went to the door and called Katy. She and the dog were busy digging in the dirt beside the woodshed.

"Come on in, Kates, and bring Samantha."

I grabbed the note and read it. It was from Kay and Isabelle explaining that they had toured the lodge and taken a few small things from the kitchen. They wanted us to come to town and pick up a table we'd already decided we didn't want. In exchange they wanted a large, ornate mahogany table they had left when they moved. There were several other items they wanted as well. Could Tom and I deliver them soon?

I was incensed that these two women, who had guarded their privacy with threats and letters to congressmen, had the nerve to go through my house a month after we'd bought it. And, they wanted us to deliver items to Yakima that we'd already agreed were to stay. I needed a walk to calm myself down.

Katy and I left the house and walked the quarter mile with Samantha to the Goose Prairie Inn. I bought Katy a snack and she and Sam went outside to visit the horses in the corral beside the store. I sat at the counter, ordered tea, and relayed the story to Darlene, one of the Inn's owners, who wasn't at all surprised.

"I was in the basement of our house one day," she said, "and I heard footsteps upstairs. I thought it was Denny and called hello. When there wasn't any answer, I decided to go up and see what was going on. There they were, those two women, looking through all of our things as if they had a right to be in our living room without an invitation. I was stunned and asked them to leave. They didn't think a thing about it and weren't embarrassed in the least. Imagine those two, who wouldn't let us step one foot on their property without raising a stink, thinking they could go through our house!"

So, it wasn't the first time they had taken liberties with other people's property. How was I going to confront them about being in our house, knowing they probably wouldn't feel embarrassed or ill at ease? Still, I didn't want to come home again and find they had been snooping around. I had to put a stop to any surprise visits.

When Tom came home later that evening we talked about the surprise visitors and their demands. I believed we had done enough for Kay and Isabelle and to give in to them now might, in the coming months, lead them to think they could come again and ask for household items. What nerve they had to be asking for furniture and other items when they hadn't fulfilled the terms of the purchase agreement on their part?

"They promised us a guest list and we haven't seen it yet," I said, knowing that Tom had asked them about this.

"No, and I don't think we will. I've talked to them several times and they say they are getting it ready. I don't believe there is one."

"But that was one of the stipulations of the sale." My sense of fairness was offended by this visit and the ensuing request.

Tom listened intently. "I think they have a list, but the people on it are as old as them or older and maybe even dead. I think we want people a little livelier than *dead* as guests!" Tom's sense of humor about all this helped bring some perspective. The women were living with the thoughts of business years ago, and we were living with the reality.

We decided to ignore their written request and say no if it was brought up again. I had invited them to come anytime, but had meant when we were home. I began locking the doors hoping it would deter them if they came to the lodge when we weren't there. Our lack of an answer seemed to take care of the problem. We never heard about it again.

Chapter Nine

TAKE IT BACK TO FRANCE

One afternoon, after the infamous visit from Kay and Isabelle, I went outside to play with Samantha. The backyard sloped steeply downward, and, from the back porch, I threw her beloved tennis ball out into the forest below. As soon as the ball was in the air, she ran full speed down the hill and into the dense underbrush. Her tail stood up like a surrender flag as she searched. She took much longer than usual to bring the ball back and when she brought it to me, it was covered with a slimy, gray liquid. She had trouble holding it in her mouth and it smelled of decay. She dropped it and I looked more closely at the disgusting blob sitting in front of me. The coating on it wasn't anything I had seen before. Probably an old rain puddle or something, I thought. Decaying leaves and old animal excrement.

I got a piece of newspaper from the house and went back out to pick up the ball.

"A new tennis ball is called for, Sammy." Her eyes never left my hand as I carried the ball, gray stuff seeping through the newspaper.

"We'll get another one and start over." The ball slid around inside the newspaper and I dropped it once or twice before getting it to the trash can.

I threw the new ball way out over the area where I thought the puddle was and she brought it back each time, the only moisture on it from her mouth.

"One last throw, girl, and then we're going in the house." We had to get Katy from the school bus stop at Whistlin' Jack Lodge, about thirty minutes drive from the ranch.

Samantha sat still, watching intently as I waved the ball in the air, pretending to toss it. She started running but stopped in place, frozen, eyes on the ball. Finally, I gave it a great throw and she was gone for a while. When she returned, the ball was once again covered with gray slime. This called for an investigation.

I walked and slid down the steep slope, catching my pants on branches, grabbing tree limbs for support. At the bottom of the hill, I headed toward the area where I thought the ball had landed. Pushing aside thorny bushes, fallen branches, and leaves, I searched for the source of the stinky, gray matter. I found it with my feet.

Solid footing gave way to wet, spongy ground. Now my sneakers were covered with slime and the odor was like potatoes, rotting in the dark corner of a deep cupboard. Pushing the bushes aside, I saw a small, rock-lined drain coming from the side of the hill.

"Oh, my gosh," I yelled at Samantha. "Our sewer is draining into the forest." My heart started pounding and my stomach gave a slight heave. I grabbed Sam and yanked her from the area. "Come on, we have to get out of this mess."

I was waiting at the door when Tom arrived home from work that evening. Extracting the two balls from the trash can, I shoved them toward him hoping for an explanation that would calm my fear of the unknown.

"What is this? Where is this stuff coming from? Is our sewer emptying into the forest?"

"Get that away from me! What are you talking about? Where did that come from?"

"I'm asking *you*." I was in a panic, not over the slime itself, but from the fear that whatever it was would cost lots of money to get rid of. We didn't have money to spend on new sewers. Poor Tom. I tend to blame him for anything I don't understand.

"Let me change my clothes, and we'll go look at it." The voice of reason and calm.

As we hiked down the back hill, Katy and Samantha thought this was quite the game. They couldn't understand the sharpness in my voice when I told them to stay put in the yard. When we reached the bottom, Tom surveyed the wet area and turned back towards the house walking into the dense brush rather than around it as we had come. He came back down, pulling bushes and long dead grasses away.

"It's a French drain."

"What's that and why weren't we told we had one?"

"It's a drain for the sinks and the clothes washer. I guess when they built the place it was legal. You'll have to throw Sammy's ball in another direction."

"What are we going to do about it?"

"For now, we're going to do nothing. The water needs to drain into the septic tank and as soon as we finish other projects, we'll fix this."

I decided to put this minor problem in the back of my mind. It still worried me because I didn't understand the complications of such a system, but Tom knew about these things and I trusted his judgment.

Chapter Ten

CAST IRON MONSTER

O ne of the more amazing pieces of equipment at the Double K Ranch was the woodstove. It was not an appliance, like a refrigerator, a modern electric oven or gas stove. Appliance implies convenience. The woodstove was many things, but convenient was not one of them. Cooking on it was time-consuming, labor intensive, grime producing and dangerous. Every part of the stove got hot when it was lit and the potential for burns increased with the temperature.

The huge, black, cast iron monster had to be reckoned with everyday and in every season. It measured three feet by eight feet and took up one whole wall of the kitchen. The stovetop was a flat grill with two circular removable burners near the stovepipe on the left side. The burners looked like manhole covers and opened to the fire below. The temperature at the end closest to the burners was blistering hot and water boiled there in a minute when the stove was fired up. Toward the other end of the stove, the grill cooled keeping a moderate simmering temperature. Below the grill top were two ovens that heated to different temperatures depending on the strength of the fire. Along the very bottom of the stove, running from one end to the other, were a series of tiny drawers into which the ash fell. At the end nearest the chimney, a larger drawer caught the hot ash dropping from the firebox above. The stove would have made a nice apartment complex for gnomes and elves.

Tom and I received minimal operating instructions from the women as part of the whirlwind maintenance tour of the property. I remembered that Isabelle had mentioned the lack of upward draw during the summer was a problem. Easy enough, I had thought, paying more attention to the attic's potential as a living space than the hole with the shiny, metal cover.

The test came one day shortly after we moved in. The afternoon was especially warm for August, but with our first guests coming in September I needed to become competent at woodstove cooking. The women had given me instructions about starting the fire.

"Start with a few small sticks and a little paper to be sure the fire takes hold before putting the larger pieces of wood in the firebox." I forgot.

I shoved in lots of paper, many sticks of varying sizes, and finally several large pieces of fir. The paper lit nicely. I closed the door and waited for the fire to roar. I was going to be a successful woodstove cook in no time! As I congratulated myself, smoke began curling out of the back panel, and then puffed out through the seams in the edges of the stove. Suddenly great clouds of dark, thick smoke shot out of the air intake on the stovepipe and a stream of bitter tasting ash shot out at me.

I yelled for Tom and rushed up the main flight of steps, opened the small door on the landing and climbed the ladder-like stairs into the attic. In the faded light from the small window at one end of the room, I found a few matches and rolled a piece of the newspaper. Yanking the silver cover from the chimney, I lit the paper, and shoved it into the hole as Isabelle had instructed. It went out. I lit another piece, pushed it into the hole, and immediately got another one and shoved it in behind the first one. I was operating on the principle that if a little is good, more is better. The paper stayed lit this time, but there was another problem. I was two stories above the kitchen and had no way of knowing whether the fire was lit. I climbed halfway down the attic stairs and yelled.

"Tom, are you there?"

"Yes." His yell back was tainted with a hint of annoyance.

I went back up the ladder and checked the newspaper. It was almost out so I lit one more, stuffed it in and lit another shoving in behind. I yelled again.

"Is it lit yet?"

"*What?*" He was annoyed and communicating this way wasn't going to help ease the tension.

"IS IT LIT YET*?*"

"*NO!*"

I put a match to more newspaper and shoved it into the hole.

"NOW?"

"*NO!*" More paper. I was down to one match.

"*OKAY!*"

"WHAT?"

"*OKAY, IT'S LIT!*"

I climbed down the attic stairs to the landing and shut the door. The pungent smoke permeated my nostrils and throat. No wonder Tom was annoyed.

The great fire lighting drama was played out on several occasions, but each time we traveled up the stairs to the attic and yelled to each other, we refined our "technique" until one match, a sheet of newspaper, and the word "okay," yelled from the attic staircase, did the trick.

Once the fire was lighted, the grill heated quickly and the cooking began. While preparing the food, I kept the fire going, placing pieces of wood in the fire box when the crackling noises slowed. The process was similar to listening for when to take the popcorn out of the microwave. There were no knobs or buttons to regulate the heat. As the fire burned in the stove, the kitchen temperature reached between 103 and 107 degrees. It continued to climb as long as the fire in the box was stoked. "*If you can't stand the heat, get out of the kitchen."* That was my motto every summer for five years!

With the coming of cold weather, the trips racing up the two flights of stairs to the attic ceased. Because of the colder air, a small fire in the firebox would blaze immediately and the stove's heat provided warmth surpassed only by the heat from the coal furnace.

On frosty winter mornings, the hot air from the stove wended its way around the railing up the stairs into the hall and bathrooms, taking with it the enticing aroma of coffee, bacon and toast being prepared. Guests, following the aroma trail, appeared at the foot of the stairs in their pajamas, asking for a cup of coffee. Some just stood at the counter dividing the kitchen from the dining room and enjoyed the mingled smells of food and wood fire. Others talked, sharing that as they lay in bed on the second floor, hearing the crackling fire and getting a whiff of breakfast, they remembered visits to grandparents when they were children.

Standing around the woodstove was like paying homage to a "god of fire." In winter, it drew people towards it, creating a place where guests became storytellers and shared aspects of themselves that they never dreamed they would disclose in public. The technical workings of a woodstove, recipes I used on it, and how much heat it generated, were topics used as conversation starters. The discussion then turned to the guests' own experiences of growing up in the Midwest or the North with a fire-powered stove providing warmth and good food. Our wood stove brought back stories of youth, campfires, and cherished family times for our guests. It held a sacred fire that brought forth memories and meaningful community times, providing comfort and, at times, healing for lonely hearts.

Chapter Eleven

WELCOMED ONCE

O ur first guests came out of the forest one day, driving an old van. They both got out of the driver's side and ambled up to the shed where I was stacking wood. The man wore a checkered shirt and jeans with streaks of dirt running down the side. The woman had on a housedress reminiscent of the early fifties. The lack of some teeth, and hair that looked like it hadn't been combed in several days, made their ages hard to guess.

"Howdy, ma'am. The folks at the store down on the road told us you might have a place for us to stay one weekend in September. We're gettin' married at the campground about a mile from here and want to spend our honeymoon night somewhere other than our van." He gave a little nervous hiccup of a laugh revealing more spaces where his teeth had been. "We're from the other side of the mountains, but we like the forest on this side. Lots drier."

The woman, with long stringy hair, talked as if she were a fourteen-year-old on a first date, her voice breathy and soft, as she looked up at her husband-to-be.

"We'd like to stay the second weekend in September. That is, if your place is takin' guests."

"I can certainly check the reservation book and see if that weekend is available." I still had to preach at church in town on Sundays and needed to check with Tom to see if he could cook Sunday breakfast.

"Come in and let me show you the room. It only has a double bed, but the view is very beautiful and you'll have the bathroom to yourselves."

As they got closer to me, I realized their clothing smelled like smoke and their teeth were stained with tobacco.

"We ask for payment at the time of booking to reserve the room, and we don't allow smoking in the bedrooms or in the lodge itself. You are welcome to smoke outside as long as you are careful and use an ashtray."

"Oh, that's not a problem. She doesn't let me smoke in our house anyway."

"You have a house already?"

"Yeah, we've been living together awhile. Thought we'd get married now. We're going to have the ceremony at the Bumping Lake Campground, like I said, and we're bringing a set of speakers that's gettin' hooked up to the car engine. We'll just put 'em up on top of the car and let it rip."

Let it rip? This was not how I imagined my first encounter with guests. People who came to the Double K were going to be educated, enjoy the outdoors in its natural state, and would have all their teeth. But, money was money, and as long as they were able to pay ahead of time, I was willing to have them.

I cleared the date with Tom and took the reservation fee. As they drove down the driveway, I felt a twinge of guilt. I was sure they were very nice people and, if I was going to be a good innkeeper, I needed to get over my desire to have only people with whom I felt comfortable. But in my heart I was hesitant.

Two weeks later, the wedding weekend arrived and we were ready to receive guests. Knowing we had one couple on this weekend and several other parties booked over the next few months created a feeling of euphoria. We were going to be successful as a retreat place that nurtured peoples' inner spirits. I looked over the living and dining rooms with pride.

The dining room floor polished just that morning, was so shiny I could see the table reflected in it. The picture windows were spotless and the sunlight poured into the space, making it warm and inviting. Clean glassware stood on the counter waiting to be filled with water and iced tea. Tom worked in the kitchen putting utensils away and making sure that the counters, sinks and stovetop were clean and clear of clutter.

Tom and I had agreed we would always sit down and have dinner with our guests since we were inviting them into our home to share a lifestyle, as well as the beautiful surroundings and lodge. So the table closest to the window was set with four new cobalt blue placemats, color-coordinated with our china. The newly purchased stainless steel flatware gleamed next to the napkins that matched the placemats. In the center of the table, a large vase overflowed with fall leaves and flowers gathered from the forest that afternoon.

Shortly after five p.m. the newlyweds arrived. They wore clothing similar to what they had worn the first day we met them, but neater and cleaner. Both had their hair combed and the bride had flowers in hers. Her dress was long and I immediately thought of "Mama Cass" and halfway expected them to break into a chorus of "Flower Girl."

After a few minutes of awkward conversation, Tom took them to their room while I finished preparing dinner. We had prepared large steaks and all the trimmings as a celebration, not only of their wedding, but also in honor of booking our first paying guests. They came to the table, I served dinner, and we all sat down to eat.

I am usually quite good at making light conversation. I tried, but they only spoke to us briefly and then gazed at each other. Tom ate faster and faster, and I thought I was sounding like some kind of out-of-kilter talking doll. I got up and cleared the dishes while Tom stood at the sink and slowly washed them.

"Why don't you go and get Katy, Tom. I can finish up here." She was at the neighbor's house and this would give him a chance to get out.

"Great. I'll be back soon." Oh, sure, I thought.

I made coffee and put the dessert on plates.

"Would you like to have your dessert in the living room? It's quite peaceful and I'm sure you'll be more comfortable sitting in there." I'll be more comfortable with you sitting in there, I thought.

"Okay. Thanks." They left the room hand-in-hand, eye-to-eye, confirming my decision to serve dessert in the other room to them alone.

I brought the cake and the coffee into the living room and set it on the table.

"Help yourselves, and if you need anything else, please let me know." They nodded, but were once again enraptured with each other as they snuggled close on the sofa.

I finished cleaning the kitchen and went down to the apartment leaving the door open a crack. If they needed me, I would hear them. An hour later when Tom and Katy finally came back, the honeymoon couple had gone upstairs to their room.

I washed the dessert dishes, set the table for breakfast and got a snack for Katy. We closed the apartment door and sat down together to watch a movie since the generator was running for the guests. When ten o'clock came, I checked in the living room to see if the happy couple had come back downstairs. They hadn't, and it was very quiet otherwise. I walked down to the garage and turned the generator off for the night.

Early the next morning, I got ready for church and made coffee for Tom and our guests. I had to leave immediately, and after giving Tom last-minute instructions, I grabbed my sermon, went out the door, got in the car, and headed to town.

I returned early in the afternoon. The newlyweds' car was gone and I found Tom sitting at the dining room table reading the newspaper. He glanced up at me and said, "If all the guests are going to be like them, they were our first and they will be our last."

"Why? What happened?"

"They came down for breakfast and never said more than three words. I decided that I wasn't going to have breakfast with them, so I served it at the living room table."

"Were they rude?"

"No, they just never said anything. After breakfast, they went back upstairs and about an hour later, they left."

"Did they say goodbye or anything?"

"Yeah, goodbye, but that was it. They were strange."

"They were on their honeymoon. I think we were probably strange on our honeymoon." He rolled his eyes around and stood up, announcing the end of the conversation.

I went upstairs to get the sheets and clean the room. It smelled like smoke. The two chairs in the bedroom were side-by-side at the window and both windows were wide open. The bottom of the wastebasket was filled with cigarette butts. I was angry. Smoking in a wooden house in the forest where fire protection is an hour away is dangerous. I had made it very clear that we didn't allow smoking inside the lodge.

I stomped downstairs to share the news with Tom, which made him sure about one thing.

"No more honeymooners." Tom's statement was emphatic.

"They won't all be like this, I'm sure."

"How can you be sure?"

"Well, I can't be absolutely sure, but we'll know the next time. And we won't take anyone who just comes out of the forest."

"Yeah, because there isn't going to be a next time. No honeymooners. No weirdoes."

We never had anyone else who wanted to use the Double K for his or her honeymoon night. But this couple did come back two years later. I heard a vehicle coming around the driveway and went out the kitchen door to see who it was. It was the brown van. This time they both got out of their own side door. She waved as soon as she saw me.

"Remember us? We were here a couple of years ago on our honeymoon night."

"Yes, I remember." I stood still outside the kitchen door, not moving any closer to greet them.

"We want to know if we can come this September and stay another night to have a little anniversary get-away."

"We're booked all of September." I didn't move toward them. They stopped moving toward me.

"What about October then?"

"Nope. Booked all of October, too." I could see the wastebasket of cigarette butts and the open window in my mind and I remembered Tom's emphatic statement.

They stood quietly, and then looked at each other.

"Okay, well thanks, maybe another time." They turned, got in the van and backed down the drive.

If these folks had been the kind of people I thought should be my kind of guests, I probably would have given them another chance. But my judgmental attitude, colored with the cigarette butt incident, didn't allow it. I had, in this encounter, come up against my own prejudice.

Chapter Twelve

ENVIRONMENTAL CLEAN-UP

In early October, we began to pay more attention to the grounds near the buildings. Around the garage we found decayed tree branches leaned precariously against old car seats and rusty fenders. Pieces of bent metal and rounds of baling wire were scattered carelessly on the ground. There was a pile of corroded scrap alongside the dirt drive and falling on it in winter might be disastrous. It was a miniature version of what we had found in the garage. We grabbed a few of the smaller scraps and threw them into the SUV to take to the dump. Larger pieces lay underneath.

The last was biggest and had sharp edges along one side. As we lifted it, I noticed the soil underneath was a rich, dark black, almost shiny.

"Lots of dead leaves under there." I was impressed with the composted dirt. Tom took a closer look.

"It's motor oil. They've been dumping motor oil on the property."

He stood looking at it for sometime before he spoke again.

"Great environmentalists, huh?"

"I guess they just didn't know. It doesn't look fresh. Maybe it has been here for awhile."

"Don't know, but we have to get rid of all the oily soil and everything around it."

"How are we going to do that?"

"We're going to dig all of it up until the ground is clear for a good number of feet. Then we'll have to haul it to the hazardous waste dump. As if we need something else to do."

The digging started that day and continued every day for two weeks until we hit soil that was clean. The oil hadn't affected the trees next to the site as far as we could see and brush grew fairly close to the spot as well. Perhaps its effect on nature in the area wasn't as bad as we thought, but it did cause certain wariness in our minds as we continued to work around the property.

We noticed a series of fence posts dotting the perimeter of the field in front of the barn. Tom thought we ought to pull them out of the ground since most of them were rotten and didn't have any fencing attached. We decided to start on the post furthest from the driveway, in an area we hadn't explored closely.

As I walked to the first post on the far side of the field, my foot caught on something and I heard cloth rip. When I bent over to free my pant leg, I found a large string of barbed wire. I picked it up and began coiling the sharp, rusted fencing, believing it was a small forgotten piece left behind. But it was long.

Tom called from the post he was working on. There was barbed wire lying in the grass there, as well.

"We need to walk this field and make sure we find it all."

"Katy and the dogs have been playing here."

I couldn't believe Kay and Isabelle had left all this barbed wire lying around in the grass. They were so particular about what everyone else did but apparently didn't hold themselves to the same standard. Their presence was being felt once again, even though they weren't physically at the ranch.

We worked for several days, coiling wire, cutting it down from around tree trunks where, in place of a post, it had been wrapped. When we were finished we probably had enough to re-fence the whole field. We pulled the posts, dragged them out of the field, and added them to the woodpile for winter. The field, cleared now, stood fresh and new, waiting for winter's cover of snow and spring's healing sunlight.

Weeks later, I found a picture album Kay and Isabelle had left behind on a bookshelf. It was small with photos of a group of executives from General Electric in Pittsburgh, Pennsylvania. In one picture, Kay and Isabelle, looking proud and robust, sat on a rugged wooden fence, which surrounded a field of thriving grasses. Horses grazed in the background near a stand of trees. I recognized it as the field where we had spent days clearing debris. The ranch in the picture had a whole different look about it. The trees, the horses, and the guests looked young, full of energy, and ready for adventure.

That ranch didn't exist now. The trees were old and majestic, the horses were gone, and the few guests I had seen from recent pictures were wrinkly and bent. It occurred to me that age had crept up on the Double K women. And so, barbed wire lay on the ground, new grass hiding its sharp existence, while the once straight posts, yielded to the push of wind, rain and snowfall.

Chapter Thirteen

LIGHT MY FIRE

It was a daunting task getting ready for winter that first fall. Being a back-woods novice, I had no idea what kinds of fossil fuel we would need or, how much, to make it through the harshest season. In my excitement about moving to the ranch I hadn't even considered our requirements for energy supplies come winter. Tom had a better grasp of the nature of our needs, but with moving, taking care of every day basic problems like getting Katy to school, figuring out the generator and water system, while holding down a fulltime job in town, he hadn't had much time to plan.

Fortunately, most of the fuel merchants had made deliveries to the Double K long before we even knew it existed. They were helpful in terms of a timetable on deliveries and how long the fuel would need to last until they could make a delivery the following spring.

The ranch operation used five kinds of fossil fuel: propane, gasoline, diesel, coal, and wood. The propane tank had been filled immediately after we arrived and the deliveryman warned us that by the end of October or maybe early November, if the weather held off, we would have to fill the thousand-gallon tank behind the house again. After that time, he wouldn't be able to make it through the rain or snow-drenched lane with the heavy truck. We scheduled the latest date he believed was safe from early season snow and hoped we would have enough money to pay for it all at once. With two gaslights, two small propane refrigerators and a set of gas burners like the kind used for camping, a thousand gallons would last until our next delivery in May. So we hoped.

The next concern was gasoline and diesel. The small generator used gasoline and provided electricity for the pump in the well house. Each time the pump needed power, it sent a signal to the small generator and it turned on automatically. I didn't understand how the whole thing worked, but when we wanted water at the house for cooking or washing, I was glad it did. To me, it seemed like magic. The large generator, which we used sparingly, ran on diesel fuel. If the ranch had guests, we provided light for three or four hours and turned it off by ten p.m.

Each thousand-gallon tank, one for diesel, one for gasoline, could be filled in mid-October but not again until the end of May because of the substantial amount of snow that fell from the steeply pitched roof onto the driveway during the winter.

A weekend thrill for our family was having the diesel generator run most of a Saturday. We washed clothes, dried sheets, and watched movies while huddled together on the couch, tucked under a quilt, eating popcorn. Katy got to be quite the movie expert during those cozy evenings especially in the classics like "High Noon," "The Philadelphia Story," and "Paint Your Wagon." We had to be sure we had enough fuel for that little pleasure.

The first year we were overly cautious with fuel consumption and kept a list of the hours and amount of gallons burned. We had some left over in May when the delivery was made. I considered that a miracle similar to the "fishes and loaves" in the New Testament or the burning oil of the Macabees in the Old.

Coal, our third fossil fuel, was delivered in late September while the ground was still firm and the hard rains hadn't started. An odd-looking red truck, small and compact, with a funnel-like structure on the top, brought five tons at a time. An equally odd looking man was the delivery person. He was short, very thin and bony, and seemed to have coal dust permanently imbedded in the skin of his face and hands. The area around his eyes was especially dark, making them look sunken and eerie. He wore overalls, high-top work boots, and carried gloves. He was old, but ageless.

The routine was the same with each delivery. He maneuvered the truck delicately between the trees, then back as close to the house as he could get without running the truck into the front stairs and porch. A small opening in the concrete wall below the front door led to the coal room, a corner of the basement cordoned off with large pieces of wood to keep the coal in one area of the cellar.

After getting out of the truck, he worked very slowly, pulling out the deep, narrow shoots from under the truck, fixing them in place after positioning them at the small opening as best he could. He pushed a lever, raising and tilting the funnel structure. The black lump coal, all shapes and sizes, clattered down the metal shoot, sometimes tumbling over the sides into the yard, thick black dust shooting up and around the truck as the coal moved faster and faster to its destination in the basement. And then the rumbling sound ceased, replaced with the whirring motor lowering the funnel-bin down into the truck again. When the coal-covered invoice was signed, I wished him a good day and he always responded with a mumble as he got in the truck and drove off.

Wood, thirteen cords a year, was the fuel that caused us the greatest trouble, yet was the one that kept us warm in our apartment, allowed us to cook for guests, and helped start up the coal furnace. Moving into the lodge in late August put us behind in gathering and chopping. We had plenty of wood from downed trees on the property, but equipment-wise we were unprepared. The shed next to the apartment had to be filled with wood thirteen inches long for the tiny fireplace in the apartment. It was our only source of heat and because it was an open fireplace, the wood burned quickly. Tom told Katy and me that we had to fill the woodshed from floor to ceiling and even then he wasn't sure that amount would be enough to get us through the winter. Every weekend he herded us into the forest and we picked up scattered branches from previous years cuttings, chopped it into pieces and flung it into the back of the SUV to be unloaded and stacked in the sheds.

I made fun of Tom's perfection in stacking wood until I realized that unless it was done that way there wouldn't be enough space for the amount of wood we needed. We collected, chopped, flung and stacked weekend after weekend, but the shed didn't look any fuller than when we had started. We finally bought several cords of wood and had them delivered, an expense we really couldn't afford monetarily, but something we had to do if we were going to survive our first winter.

The two-foot long logs for the massive fireplace in the lodge great room were stacked on the sides of the front porch steps. Tom cut pieces off logs with his new chain saw, and then I used an axe, wedge and sledgehammer to make them a size that we could lift and fit into the fireplace. Since the apartment was a priority, we didn't cut too much of this larger size, but we needed enough to create heat and ambiance for the guests. This was the hardest work I had ever done in my life and it gave me new respect for pilgrims and pioneers. In bed at night, after chopping wood all day then lifting it into our vehicle, my muscles and joints pleaded for a reprieve from the torturous work. I silenced them with large doses of aspirin or ibuprofen.

After several weekends of this I asked Tom how people who lived in the valley below us cut all the wood I saw stacked near their homes. I never saw them out on their property working this hard.

"They have wood splitters."

"What's a wood splitter? Aren't I using wood splitters?" I had never heard of such a thing.

"No, I'm talking about wood splitters that have engines. You set a large piece of log on a narrow metal platform, start the engine and it pushes the wood into another piece of sharp heavy metal, like a giant axe head. It splits the wood. You just keep putting the pieces on it until they're all split into the size you want them to be."

"Why don't we have one of those?"

"Because they cost about two thousand dollars and we don't have the money."

"What if we got a used one?" My aching body was cheering me on.

"Who, up here in the woods, is going to sell their wood splitter?" Good question.

My mission in the next few months would be to search the paper for a piece of equipment that would make our lives easier, save our bodies for future living, and free up time for other details of the business.

We continued to cut through the darkening days of fall, bringing in what we thought was enough wood for the kitchen stove. We used Douglas fir, a much denser wood, in the kitchen, which provided a more intense heat.

The kindling wood for the big furnace in the basement had to be a certain length to fit inside, but we could also use scrapes, odd branches, and anything else we could find on the property to get us through this first winter.

We made Katy collect wood, small pieces for kindling in the kitchen. She gathered it into one place and then sat on a stump and broke it into the sizes her father measured for her. Her attitude towards this process darkened, as the days grew shorter and our concern for being prepared for winter increased. She sat on her stump and mumbled hateful words about being at the Double K and the work we made her do. She wanted to live with her six-year old friends in Yakima.

I felt guilty and troubled by her behavior. Having to move far away from friends, go to a new school, ride a bus to school for an hour and a half each way, and put up with the lack of electricity and centralized heating at home was difficult. But I had never heard her say she hated something and that statement created a measure of doubt in my mind about the purchase of the Double K.

She probably understood, in a six-year-old-way, that expressing hatred was the instrument which hurt me the most. She was in pain because of the move and she wanted me to share some aspect of it.

Give it time, I thought. She'll make friends and will be her old self again. We were too involved preparing for the coming snow and cold to allow her or ourselves much self-pity. I felt the same about all this hard work, but I couldn't complain. I was the one who had desperately wanted to be at the Double K.

Chapter Fourteen

EMERGENCY QUICK FIX

M ost weekends during fall we had single guests or couples who stayed one night or occasionally, two. Huge amounts of energy went into cleaning the lodge. When I figured what I was being paid by each guest for all my hours of scrubbing, washing and waxing, frustration overwhelmed me. Working to get the place fixed up both inside and out, making an extra effort for each guest, as well as meal preparation, left me exhausted. There had to be some profit, even if miniscule. I was beginning to think I had made a gross miscalculation in terms of what the ranch could provide in income.

The ranch was getting labeled as a bed and breakfast and that was not what we intended. Because of the money and the recommendations I hoped each visitor would pass along, all were welcomed. We didn't have a lot of time and we needed every penny of income I could produce.

I kept a good spirit most evenings but during the night lay awake, the worry eating away at my gut. Once in a while, after Tom went to sleep, I cried. My dream of what life should be like at Goose Prairie had finally locked horns with the reality. I needed Tom, as the realist, to tell me the truth. One evening, feeling ready to hear what he had to say, I ventured into the arena.

"I'm worried the lodge isn't bringing in enough money each month."

Tom was plain spoken. "We've got some savings, but that's going rapidly and we've got the fuel to pay for as well as our regular bills."

"I wanted to have groups," I told him. "We've had couples and individuals instead. Cleaning for one person or two just doesn't make any sense. I'm spending great amounts of energy for very little return."

After much discussion, we began to develop a plan.

"We could have a group rate," I said, "but the group would have to be six or more. That would guarantee a certain amount of money, and the work I'm doing would be the same since I clean the whole place for one or ten. If the rate is cheap enough, we could get groups that might not otherwise choose to come to a retreat."

Tom thought for a while. He'd had lots of experience figuring out fair prices for scout camp including food, utilities and all the related costs. He jotted some numbers down on a piece of paper, did some figuring and then replied.

"If we had six per night and they stayed for two nights, we could charge around $40 per night and make three times what we make with one or two guests. I think it's worth a try."

The brochure I made when we began marketing the ranch had a separate price sheet, so all I had to do was re-do the prices. I begin distributing them to local church groups, my initial target audience. Sparks of excitement came back and I felt enthusiastic once again.

Within a week, we had a reservation from a churchwomen's group in the lower Yakima Valley. I had been their interim pastor at one time and felt they were doing it to help me out. At this point, I was willing to accept charity. It was for one night only, but sixteen people were coming and that made cleaning and preparation less tedious.

The big day arrived. The floors were spotless, dust was nowhere to be seen, and the windows sparkled. The group arrived at 2 p.m. one late October afternoon, and following some simple refreshments, they adjourned to the great room for a meeting. Their laughter and conversation thrilled me. This is what I had envisioned.

The women seemed to enjoy the atmosphere, although some of them, being older, complained about climbing the steps to the bathrooms during the break. I could hear toilets flushing at a fairly constant rate and then silence as the group meeting started up again.

I went to the corner of the dining room where the great room joined it, the two separated by a narrow wall, and peeked in to make sure the women were comfortable. The light was fading and the older ladies were having trouble seeing the pages they were reading. I realized the generator need to be turned on earlier than usual to keep this group happy.

As I turned to go, I caught a whiff of something smelly. Water was running down the narrow wall on the dining room side. I wasn't sure where it was coming from, but the puddle on the floor, told me it had been happening for a while. As I watched, the water slowed to a trickle and then stopped. As one of the women went up the stairs to the use the bathroom, the realization hit me. The bathrooms were up above the wall. Sure enough, when the toilets were flushed, water ran down the wall again. The smell, which had dissipated, returned. I stood by the wall as a woman came down the stairs. I smiled and greeted her, hoping she wouldn't see the mess.

Many old newspapers and paper towels later, the water on the floor was gone. I wiped the walls down with disinfectant. When was Tom going to get here? I couldn't keep the floor and wall dry, help them, fix dinner, and start the generator at the same time. And I didn't really want to start the generator while the water was dribbling down the wall. I stood, frozen by the inability to decide what to do next.

"Kathleen." I was startled by the voice. It was the group leader. "We need more light. The older women are complaining because they can't see the pages we're reading. Could you turn on the generator now?"

"Sure. As soon as I get dinner to a point where I can leave it, I'll get it started." I busied myself in the kitchen while keeping an eye on the wall across the room. Then I heard Tom's car in the driveway. What a relief. From the kitchen window I saw a truck pull up behind him. It was the camp ranger, Richard. What luck and good timing!

Katy waved and shouted as she jumped down from the front seat and slammed the vehicle's door hard. She ran into the kitchen, letting the door bang behind her. She gave me a big hug, paused, studied the dining room wall then practically shouted, "What is all that water running down the wall?"

"Shhhh... I need your Dad to come look at it without the women knowing. Why don't you go in the living room and say hello to them while I talk to him?" The women knew her from church and she viewed many of them as adopted grandmas.

As they came in the door, I explained the situation to Tom and Richard. Something had to be done before the ladies came in for the meal. Dinner with a waterfall of toilet waste was not going to be a highlight for these prim and proper members of the Women's Association.

"Can you turn on the generator so we can see what's going on here?" asked Tom.

I was so concerned about the women seeing the water and smelling the odor I had completely forgotten about the lights. I went down to the generator house in the garage, and primed the engine. It started easily, which was not its habit. Perhaps it knew that now was not the time to act up. I trudged back to the house in the darkness, scolding myself for not paying more attention to the needs of the guests.

When I came in the back door, Tom, still in his business suit, was climbing the ladder and Richard in his heavy coat stood below trying to see what was wrong. They took a small section out of the ceiling, which revealed the plumbing above. A sewer pipe with a "Y" at the top ran along the inside of the paneling to the bathroom on the second floor. A circular piece of wood, cut from a small tree trunk or huge limb, was stuffed in the hole where a rubber plug should have been. And, it was all held together with baling wire. The water from the toilets had eaten away at the wood and it no longer provided a tight seal. At that moment, what had seemed to me a monumental problem took on a hint of comedy.

The presence of Kay and Isabelle were visiting us at this most inopportune time. The old wire from the horses' hay bales held together so many parts of the ranch: pipes leading to the chimney from the furnace, the muffler of the small generator, door and window closures in the basement, lights strung up in the garage, wobbly fences held to rotting fence posts, and now this piece of tree shoved in the sewer pipe. All held up, down, or together with baling wire.

The men quietly discussed a temporary fix for the problem. Richard left and a short time later arrived back with some rubber material he had gotten from the Boy Scout camp. He and Tom removed the wood, stuffed some rags into the holes and wrapped the plug pieces with the rubber.

"As makeshift as *their* solution," Tom said, shoving the tree trunk slices, now wearing tight black rubber around their middles, back in the holes. "But I'll remember to get to the hardware store and replace this with the real thing next time I'm in town. Kathleen, can you go upstairs and flush a few times? We'll see if this works."

I climbed the stairs to the second floor, flushed each toilet twice, and heard the "okay." This was an easy fix. Now I could concentrate on dinner and the group, rather than water pouring down the wall.

Tom, still in his suit, washed down all the surfaces with sanitizer and bleach, mopped the floor with the same solution, and sprayed disinfectant to ease the smell.

"Not many men show up for their night job in a fancy suit."

"Only the best for you, dear. Only the best."

Humor was proving to be the baling wire of our life at the ranch. In light of all that had happened so far, I hoped lots of it was still lying around.

Chapter Fifteen

EARLY SNOW

One morning in late October, as light crept over the hillside, Tom and Katy went out the kitchen door laughing and talking, and found themselves surrounded by elk of all sizes. Two bulls stood at either end of a large herd of cows and babies. Chaos ensued. The babies rushed around screaming for their mothers, while the mothers took to the hill behind the house, or ran down the driveway and crossed the field until they were under cover of the trees.

Tom and Katy froze in the driveway while I stood silently at the back door. The sounds of scattering elk ceased and just as suddenly the air was filled with the pitiful wailing of the babies separated from the herd. Every few seconds, there was an answer to the babies' cries.

Eventually, Tom climbed into the SUV, buckled Katy in, and drove down the driveway. I closed the back door gently and went to the living room windows. From the surrounding forest, the wailing sounds grew louder. Elk started to appear, walking cautiously out of the trees, sounding a gathering call to the rest of the scattered herd. Babies ran towards the sounds, listened and then turned in a different direction, as if following a siren. Tree branches snapped, and fallen leaves, crisp and dry, crunched under the hooves of the moving animals. The sounds became quieter, until I was left in silence again.

Each morning we experienced some version of this escapade but to a lesser degree. We learned to move more quietly so we wouldn't startle the elk, and they learned not to come as close to the house at that time of day.

The herds were moving to lower elevations searching for food, while on the far mountainsides, the snow line crept lower and lower. When the line was at 12, 000 feet we experienced only a chill in the air. But, by the time the weather report said the snow level was at 5,000 feet, the wet, cold wind told us it wouldn't be long before snow would fall on us as well.

The first snow fell overnight early in November. I woke, climbed down from the loft and stared out the window by the foot of the stairs. White puffs balanced on the ends of the evergreen branches and the birds on the feeder danced around the wooden edges trying to clear the snow off the bird seed I had put out the day before. I sat on the couch for a while, waiting for the light of morning to brighten.

Snow, I thought. It's too early for snow. But then again, by whose calendar is it too early? Mine? Why should mine count? I could fight against the snow, to no avail, or I could reflect on it and allow its beauty to teach me something about living in nature without trying to change it. Easy to ponder, hard to embrace.

Two small chipmunks scurried over the back rail interrupting my thoughts. Throughout the autumn months I had noticed the little animals running back and forth over the top of the woodpile around the side of the house, across the deck and up the pole holding the bird feeder. With tails held aloft, sounding a ch-ch-cheeting noise as a warning, and stuffing their mouths with a few chosen goodies from the feeder, they had scurried back down and run off in the same direction they had come. This process was repeated many times. Mouths empty, mouths full, mouths empty again.

One morning I went out the front door just as one tiny, striped chipmunk came around the corner by the front porch. His little cheeks were puffed out like saddlebags on the side of a horse. Stopping short as he saw me, he tried to go left across the woodpile, but I stepped left to see what he would do. He headed to the right. I stepped right, a quick two-step. The chipmunk finally sat down, looked at me and tried one more time, a repeat of the dance. The little fellow stopped and glared. His tail went high into the air and puffed out like a hairy blowfish. I thought the chipmunk was going to leap his way across me. Instead, he turned and ran in the opposite direction. I sat quietly on the porch step waiting, but the furry creature didn't return.

Now, as the snow fell outside the window, I realized the seriousness of the chipmunk's behavior. He had been preparing himself for what lay ahead, while I had played idle games.

The forecast on Public Radio had called for two or three feet of snow, but only three or four inches had fallen. It was still coming down lightly, and icicles were dropping off the roof gutters from the weight of the snow further up.

As I sat watching the last few flakes of this storm's snow, I knew our family would now enter another phase of mountain life. Snow meant the hard work outside had to stop. Darkness and silence surrounded us more each day and brought a certain level of excitement. But some trepidation at what this season would bring, and how we as a family would cope with all the changes, stood between us, unspoken.

Chapter Sixteen

NEIGHBORLY ASSISTANCE

As our family established a daily routine there was a feeling of comfort with the sameness of each day. At the same time, the fear of unknown conditions we might face in bad weather, and a lack of preparedness in spite of all the preparations we had made, seeped in every once in a while. Sadness accompanied joy as we realized that friends were now far away and wouldn't be coming to see us as often as before. With the work we had at the ranch, we wouldn't be partying in town.

I carried a heavy pack of these emotions along with me and weight was added to it by the thought that I had taken on the ranch, a huge project I couldn't handle. Someone might find out I was more scared than I let on, which would, in my mind's eye, expose a great weakness in my character.

This was not the result of moving to Goose Prairie. Anxiety had tagged along all my life. But the solitude of living at the ranch, the constant wrangling with situations we had not ever imagined, as well as my inability to "read" the feelings of people around us as we settled into this new life, was raising its level to new heights.

From what I had seen and heard, my perception of the Goose Prairie permanent community of twelve, which included the three of us, was one of "see if they make it through the winter then befriend them." I didn't object to that. Too many people had grandiose ideas about living in the wilderness and then were gone by the second snowfall. I didn't want to be one of those. Rather, I desperately wanted to be seen as strong and ready to meet any challenge. I wanted to prove myself worthy of their friendship and I wanted to be a *member* of this little group. Added to that desire was the overtime my imagination and intuitive nature were putting in.

I believed that Richard, the camp ranger, was not pleased that we had moved to Goose Prairie. I felt he thought I would need to enlist his help in matters of the ranch all the time. I had avoided doing too much manual labor around the Boy Scout Camp during the summers preceding our move. I had Katy, who was a toddler at the time, and truthfully considered being at camp a vacation. I wasn't there to work. I think, too, Richard was a little concerned about having Tom, his employer, so close by.

One evening when Tom was traveling in the northern part of the state, I heard on the radio the temperature was going to drop rapidly. By 9 p.m., it would be –20 degrees.

Going to the basement, I loaded the furnace with enough coal to last throughout the night. Next, I built the biggest fire I could in our apartment fireplace so the heat might linger after we had gone to bed. The tiny fireplace was totally inadequate, but it was all we had. In our postage stamp bathroom, I turned the water on slightly creating a drip in the shower and sink, switched on the gaslight to provide a little extra heat, and headed to the living room. Starting a huge fire in the great room fireplace, I crushed newspaper, threw it in the big fireplace, topped that with kindling and large two-foot logs, and lit it. Katy settled on the couch and the dogs stretched out nearby.

"I've got to get the heater going in the well house, sweetheart, so you stay here with the dogs and I'll be back as soon as I can." If she really needed me I would be down the hill, a holler away.

Dressing in insulated underwear, warm clothes and thick, down outerwear, I put on a heavy wool cap, pulled it down around my ears, wrapped a scarf around my face and headed out the front door. The well house was a short walk from the lodge and since the generator was running, there was enough light for me to see my way around and down the driveway without a flashlight. At the well-house, I opened the door quickly, ducked in and shut it behind me, switching on the single light bulb fixture to see what I had to do.

The heater inside was small and electric. Each time the little generator came on to run the pump, the heater would start and heat the room. The water in the house was on slow drip so that even when we were sleeping the pump would have to run on a fairly regular basis.

This is ingenious, I thought, as I pushed the heater's plug into the socket on the side of the light bulb fixture. I had some concern about the room getting too hot, but I doubted it was airtight and at -20 degrees the heater would have to put out some pretty fierce rays to get the place too hot. Hopefully the water was dripping enough to keep the generator operating all night. I didn't care about wasting fuel. The pipes had to stay open or we were in big trouble.

As I came out of the well-house and shut the door, I heard a truck coming up the lane. Who would be out on this night when they ought to be keeping their own home-fires burning? I began to walk toward the house, not wanting to stand outside talking to whoever was coming up the drive. The vehicle came slowly, and finally in the light of the porch lamp I saw it was the camp ranger's truck. Richard drove up and around the circle and I met him at the top of the drive.

"Thought I'd come over and tell you that the temperature's supposed to fall to -20 tonight. Do you know what to do? I can help with whatever needs to be done." Richard was here, bless his heart, to be sure I was okay while Tom was away.

"I heard that news on the radio. I think I've done everything I can."

"Have you turned the water on in the house a little bit?"

"I did that about an hour ago."

"How about the furnace? Did you stoke it?"

"First thing. And, I started a fire in the living room as well as in our apartment." So far so good. I felt like I was passing the mountaineer's beginner test.

"What about the well house? Saw you walking up from there."

"I made sure the heater was plugged in and working. It should be okay most of the night and I can get up early and check it in the morning."

He seemed pleasantly surprised that I had done everything I could to insure our comfort and safety during this abrupt cold snap. I was pleased too, and proud of myself. Maybe I wasn't such a city pansy.

"Okay," he said. "I better get home and check my own systems at camp."

"Thanks for stopping, Richard. I appreciate the reminders." I really did appreciate his thoughtfulness. What if I had forgotten something? His truck crept back down the lane until the red from the taillights disappeared entirely.

I turned, climbed the steps to the front door and entered the toasty-warm living room. This evening's activity had given me a little confidence in my ability to handle unforeseen events. I took off my hat, coat and boots, and joined Katy on the sofa, basking not only in the heat of the fire, but also in the glory of having done my mountain tasks correctly by myself.

But my satisfaction was short-lived and bittersweet. The next day Richard reported to me that while he was making sure the ranch's systems were ready for the cold, some of his pipes had frozen. I was saddened that his kindness had been repaid with more work and trouble for him.

Getting ourselves through the first frigid weather in Goose Prairie seemed to make an impression on some of the neighbors. My sense of humor about it overcame the fear, at least in public, and, I made fun of myself and my lack of mountain knowledge.

One late November afternoon, after the worst of this bout of deep cold was over, a neighbor, Webb, called to us as we were walking to the Boy Scout camp. We met at the side of the road.

"You know, I made a little wine here at the end of the summer and it's about ready for tasting. You folks in the mood for a little wine?"

I wasn't sure I was ready for wine at two in the afternoon, but I was ready to do some socializing. His cabin, which he had built from logs gathered in the forest around the property, had a small front porch. All summer long, I had admired pots filled with flowers hanging over the railings. Boxes filled with red geraniums had framed each window ledge. White curtains hanging at the windows made the red of the flowers seem more vivid. We walked into the cabin and down a short hallway into the back part of the house where the living room faced the river. Doors that opened onto a patio gave a relaxing view of the water and the forest beyond. A fire burned in the fireplace.

Webb and Sonda, the owners of this cabin, had moved to the Prairie from Tacoma. Webb had been a firefighter and he and Sonda had two grown children and several grandchildren. We had gotten to know them a little through the times at the Goose Prairie Inn before we moved, but we hadn't spent time with them alone in their house. Sonda spoke first.

"Hi, you two. I'm just getting some glasses and snacks."

"Have a seat," said Webb. "I've got the wine right outside the back door."

I headed to the big rocker facing the fireplace while Tom sat in an overstuffed chair. Webb fetched the bottle. He brought it to the table and uncorked it.

"I don't know how it will taste yet. It's a bit young, but it looks good."

The liquid he poured was deep magenta. As he filled our glasses, the aroma of the wine floated gently around the room teasing my nose and sense of taste. Sitting down, he raised his glass.

"To the Andersons and their new home here at Goose Prairie." We all raised our glasses then drank. The wine was thick and sweet and went down easily. Webb was soon filling our glasses again. The alcohol, the heat of the fire, and the conversation mingled to provide a very satisfying afternoon.

After several hours, Tom and I said our "goodbyes", thanked them for the afternoon's refreshment, and invited them to come to the ranch sometime soon. I was high not only on the drink we had shared, but on what seemed to me to be a turning point in our relationship to the people at the Prairie. Being invited to share homemade wine and conversation on a November afternoon was the start of many neighborly adventures that first year.

Chapter Seventeen

DOGS IN PARADISE

From the kitchen window I saw Tom trying to get something out of the back of the SUV. I went to see what he was doing. In the shadows lay a big black dog with huge ears pointing outward from the sides of her head like two triangles falling down opposite sides of a hill. She was skinny to the point of being sickly and lay flattened to the floor.

We tried to coax her out of the vehicle. Tom pulled her gently from the front, while I pushed her lightly in the back. When we eventually got her out onto the wet ground she immediately lay down. The rain soaked into her dark coat until she started to shiver. I was beginning to shake with the cold, too, and Tom's jacket looked like a baggy wetsuit top. We pushed and pulled until we got her through the back door and down into our small apartment.

Bear, as she was called, had lived with a family in the south part of the Yakima Valley and from all accounts had been abused. She needed a new home. When asked if we could take her, I said "Maybe." Tom decided for both of us.

Bear found a corner in the apartment close to the door. In the light, her wet coat showed the outline of each rib and the long line of her backbone. She was unwilling to look at us unless she thought we were not looking at her. And, when she did, she looked up quickly then turned her eyes to the floor again. For three days she lay on the apartment floor in the same location, not eating, but drinking the tiniest sips of water. I stopped to pet her whenever I passed and talked to her as I worked in the kitchen, three small steps up from the apartment.

Slowly she began to explore the area closest to her "spot," and when I came into the apartment her tail wiggled a little. I took her to the door when she showed signs of needing to go out but getting her to go out or come in was a chore. She was afraid of the door itself and after a few false starts bolted out as fast as she could, watching the door every second. By the end of the first week, she was following me everywhere I went except if I went in or out of a door – then I had to coax her once again.

Bear became braver and explored areas in the main lodge as she regained her strength and health and this created a small problem. She was so tall she could reach up on the counter and steal whatever was left there. One evening it was a pound of butter, later leftover meatloaf. She was quick and sneaky, but the smell of the hair around her mouth told the story. Our behavior had to change to accommodate a thief and since she was gentle and kind we made the change and simply kept her out of the kitchen.

Samantha was a small black Lab who had been with our family in Yakima and had moved to the ranch with us. I raised her from a tiny "runt of the litter" puppy into a beautiful, shiny-coated, sweet dog. She was not happy that Bear now occupied an important place in our lives. She watched Bear and Bear watched her. Neither dog wanted to have anything to do with the other. I believed they would be fine together once they knew each other better.

After a few weeks, I decided to take them on a walk together. I put Bear on a leash and Samantha, being an obedient girl, walked alongside of me. We walked down to the Goose Prairie Inn, where I had coffee and then we ambled back up the drive without incident. As we got closer to the house, Samantha walked in front of Bear. It sparked a fight. Bear attacked Samantha and the two of them engaged in battle.

I had never seen Samantha fight the way she did that day. She grabbed at Bear's ears and then lunged. Bear, the larger dog, came down on top of Samantha, biting her shoulder, trying to reach for her throat. Bear's strength had returned and now she was trying to gain first place in the pack. They tumbled around like two kids in a schoolyard brawl. I screamed at them, grabbed a dead branch, and began hitting them both. In a moment the fight was over. Sammy shook and had minor bites, which were bleeding slightly. Bear, whose hair was long and thick, showed no signs of injury. On that day, the pack's order was established and the two of them never fought again. Bear became the dominant dog and Samantha went along as the follower.

One Saturday morning Bear and Samantha disappeared. Several bicycle riders had been on our dirt lane and I thought the dogs had followed them. We found Samantha not far from the house and sent her home. But Bear was nowhere to be seen. I yelled for her around our grounds, drove around and called her name out the car window hoping she would appear from the forest near the roadway. Then I ceased the search believing she would find her way back. I hoped someone hadn't picked her up thinking her lost. I had grown to love her. She was young and still impetuous but had made so much progress in such a short time.

The day went by and we still hadn't located her. We drove further from the house, scanning the forest close to the road. No Bear. By Sunday morning she still hadn't shown up and anger swelled inside of me. I had nurtured and loved this dog back to health and jeopardized my relationship with sweet Samantha Jane. This is how Bear was repaying me? The desperately sad feeling of despair that I had not watched her carefully enough, that she would once again fall into the hands of someone who would abuse her or worse sickened me.

Early Sunday afternoon, a pick-up truck came up the dirt lane, and circled in the driveway close to the house. Who should be tied in the back but Bear! Oh, what a mixture of feelings I had at that moment – relief, anger, joy and thankfulness- mostly joy and thankfulness, I must admit. The truck's owner had found Bear at the lake playing with all the campers. Believing that the dog probably belonged to someone, he tied her up at his campsite. On his way out of Goose Prairie, he inquired at the store whether there were any reports of lost dogs and of course, there had been – Bear! We had a wonderful re-union and even Samantha seemed pleased her leader had returned.

We left the house as soon as it was light enough to see the way. I got the dogs' leashes; they did their jumping dog, tap dance routine, and sat long enough to have the leashes attached to their collars. Bear was the only one who needed the leash, but I believed Samantha felt left out if I didn't at least start her on one. We went down the dirt lane, all of us sniffing the air, coal fumes, plant smells and damp earth, which mingled to create a distinctive forest aroma. I'm sure the dogs discerned many more layers of smells than I did and if they could have talked, they would have identified all the animals and people who had passed by in the last twenty-four hours. The sky seemed to open as we reached the field at the foot of the drive. Sunlight played through the trees reflecting off snow or dew drops, twinkling at me among branches, disappearing for a moment then reappearing at the next opening.

I waited until we were far into the forest before I let Bear off the leash so she could run without hindrance. She took off through the trees, moved quickly from spot to spot, sniffing and sometimes pawing at the underbrush to get a better whiff of other animals' scat or pieces of dead animal carcass. I lost sight of her every few minutes then she circled back through the trees playfully hitting my hand to reassure me she was not running away. Off she went again, each run as exciting as the last. I think

I tested her loyalty and love each time I let her go, but something in her wild nature told me she must have that freedom.

Samantha didn't have that need and stayed close to my side or within my sight. She seemed to derive her enjoyment from being with me, sniffing the cool mountain air, and occasionally straying a short way to check out a hole or a rotten tree branch housing insects or mice. I just kept my pace and shortly she would catch up. She never lost sight of me or I of her. Our bond deepened in those long quiet walks through the forest, strengthened by the solitude of our surroundings.

Watching the dogs as I walked, I felt they represented the two sides of my feelings about living in Goose Prairie. Samantha walked silently and regally beside me and took it all in, not letting the emotion of the moment betray her feelings. I believed I had to be outwardly strong and unwavering in my enthusiasm for choosing to live in Goose Prairie no matter what I really felt at times. Bear's running through the forest, leaping at the slightest movement, sniffing furiously, or barking randomly at something in the air, reminded me of all the excitement and joy I had felt when the ranch became ours. In those moments, I knew I had chosen the right pathway for our family.

Just as we set up certain routines inside the house, the dogs set up certain ones outside. On their first early-morning jaunt they followed the perimeter line of the property surrounding the lodge. I would hear Bear barking as she treed a squirrel, found the freshly dug burrow of a mole, or ran a skunk under the barn. Sometimes the barking told me they were spending a little extra time at the barn, and later, I would see their handiwork (footwork!) They had dug deep under the barn floor trying to get to a skunk or had gouged the field hoping to ferret out a mole. When Bear and Samantha returned to the lodge, rich, dark soil covered their noses, legs and paws, and they smelled of moist earth. The same routine around the perimeter of the property was repeated at night, but they returned sooner, especially in winter, when the temperature dropped below zero.

Bear enjoyed the snowy winter. At the first snowfall, she raced out and flung herself, snout first, into whatever snow had fallen. As the snow got deeper, she rolled and dug and then flung herself even further into it until her whole body was covered. Emerging in a moment, she looked like an abominable snow monster. She loved to run in the snow, and the size of her paws which looked like snowshoes, helped her through. When she tired she lay down and the black fur against the white snow background made her look more like a Bear than a dog.

Samantha hated the snow. She would do anything to avoid it especially if it were deep. She was a dainty dog with small, slender feet and space between her claws. Snow hardened in those spaces and made it painful for her to walk. We shoveled pathways to get her out the door to do her doggie business – like shoveling a path to the outhouse.

Getting Bear solved the problem. She charged out into the snow, and being so much wider and taller than Samantha, she cleared a pathway. Bear's weight and large feet patted the snow down firmly. Sammy just followed Bear until Bear's path led back to the house. But one day the two dogs ran into a problem. Eighteen inches of snow had fallen during the night, and since the temperature was close to freezing, the snow was not as dry as usual. When I opened the door in the morning, Bear bounded out with her usual enthusiasm and Samantha followed close behind with her usual reluctance. I watched them as they made their way down the back driveway. Bear was working extra hard to get through the snow and Samantha was constantly running into her tail. Bear was not one to have anything, especially another dog, close behind her but she was patient with Samantha, and tried to move a little faster to put some distance between them. Soon neither of them moved at all. Bear was stuck and Samantha, following so closely, had no room to maneuver to turn around. They stood there in wet snow up to their chins.

I quickly put pants and a coat over my pajamas, pulled on my boots and mittens, and went to help. They stared at me without making a sound, and I wondered what was going on in their little dog brains. I moved as fast as I could, but because the snow was so heavy and deep, it took a few minutes to reach them. I dug Bear out with my hands and made her a turnaround space next to Samantha. Immediately, she knew what to do. She turned, climbed around Samantha, and headed back the way she had come. Samantha just stood there, shivering and bedraggled. I picked her up and carried her back along the narrow path I had made, put her down in the woodshed and watched as she shook herself from head to tail trying to regain her lost dignity.

When she was done, Bear arrived panting heavily and shook as well. But her shake said, "When are we doing this again? Soon?" Bear was ready for another snow adventure; Samantha for the warmth of the fireplace and the cozy rug in front of it.

Chapter Eighteen

DARKNESS, DOUBTS AND FEARS

On early winter mornings, I went down the coal dust covered steps to the basement. The floor of the cellar was dirt, which added more grime to the coal dust already covering the railings, stairs, wooden walkway to the furnace, and everything else in the basement with a flat surface. After lighting the gas lantern near the huge black cast-iron furnace, I put on a thick mitt and opened the heavy iron door. Small puffs of smoke circled around and out of the furnace, the intense heat boring through to my fingertips in spite of the heavy protective covering. Picking up the heavy metal poker and pushing what was left of the burning chunks of coal around to get a flame going again, I pulled out the clinkers, and shoveled heavy coal lumps on top of the burning bits left from the night before.

If the fire had gone out in the night, which it did occasionally when the damper was left open or the chimney had been cleaned, to create an extremely hot fire, it meant starting from scratch. First crumpled sheets of newsprint were thrown into the firebox, then kindling, and finally, a couple of larger pieces of wood. When the fire got going, I added a few smaller lumps of coal, waited until they ignited then threw in the larger ones, which weighed ten pounds or more. Closing the furnace door as the larger pieces caught fire, I headed back upstairs.

I am not a very orderly person but the routine of the fire was a simple one that focused my life when other things about the ranch, like major snowstorms, no electricity, and lack of financial security were out of my control. Each step in building the fire was easy, and the daily necessary routine of following them in order to heat the lodge brought calmness as the day began.

In winter I couldn't stay in bed and hope that someone else would "turn up the heat" as we had done at our house in town. The work of rebuilding the fire was constant, though not taxing. Still, what went along with it was arduous: slippers covered with dirt from the floor, coal dust on my robe, nightgown and hands, ashes and dust up my nose and in my mouth. Avoiding the mice scurrying around the woodpile and whacking the occasional packrat or squirrel that happened to squeeze it's way in through who knows where added a certain unique ambiance to the morning routine. I always tried to get what dirt and dust I could off my clothing and myself before going back upstairs but I had limited success as the washday water told me later in the week.

Back in the kitchen, I made coffee and lots of it. If we had guests, even more. The process was labor intensive. Boil the water on the wood stove, put it through the filter a little at a time and pour the coffee into 2-gallon thermal containers to keep it hot. I had to be "present", unlike in town where the pot came on automatically in the morning and turned itself off when it had brewed. I packed lunches for my family and the guests and then went back to the apartment to get Katy out of bed.

It was especially hard to get her up and on her way to school the first winter when she was six. The only illumination in the apartment and the loft was from the single gas light in the middle of the room. And, winter in Goose Prairie was very dark: no reflecting lights of the city, no streetlights and no sunlight until late in the morning.

The tiny fireplace while it was going strong in the apartment barely gave enough heat to maintain a temperature between thirty and forty degrees. When it went out after we had gone to bed, the air from outside quickly made its way down the chimney and cooled what little heat we did have. Mornings were often unbearably cold in the apartment when I went up the loft ladder to wake Katy.

I reluctantly urged her out from under the warm quilts into the frigid morning air. She was such a small girl for her age, not fragile, but with very little body mass to keep her warm. She was a real trooper about the process of getting out of bed, but on the coldest mornings she would cry, tell me she was sick, and beg to miss school. I knew her attitude would be better once she was dressed and fed. She really didn't like to miss school because her many friends and social life during the school day made her later isolation at Goose Prairie easier so I always said no. She had to go.

After a few hugs and kisses, I bundled her up in a blanket and carried her down the loft steps, up into the kitchen and through to the lodge living room. Putting a small blanket and a stool over the air grate of the coal furnace, I sat her on the stool. The heat would rise and circle around her like a prince until she was awakened by its gentle kiss of warmth. I laid her clothes on the grate as well. When she finally did get dressed, her little underwear and socks were toasty warm on her tiny body. After dressing, she bundled up in snow pants, boots, heavy coat, gloves and mittens. She took a good breakfast with her since there was not time to eat before leaving for school. She and her dad went out the front door and trudged down the driveway through deep snow to the truck parked in the field below the lodge.

Tom went first making a path for Katy. The light of their flashlights bobbed back and forth, back and forth, getting smaller as they got further from the house. When I no longer saw them, I partially shut the front door. Through the small crack I could hear the truck engine start, see the headlights go on through the trees and hear the doors slam shut. I closed the front door all the way and watched through the lodge living room windows for the headlights reflection to grow dimmer and finally disappear.

I walked slowly through the living room, lit by the reflection of light from the old-fashioned oil lamp, went to the kitchen, and made myself a small pot of tea. Sitting down at the kitchen counter in the bright circle of light from the gas lamp overhead, I turned on the battery-powered radio and listened to Bob Edwards and his guests on National Public Radio. So quiet. The voices and music of the radio and me listening in the middle of the wilderness.

Almost every morning in that quiet, I would reflect on the effect this monumental move to Goose Prairie was having on my daughter. Sending her off in the dark, cold and silent morning during winter was not an easy task for me. I knew she and her Dad had their own private adventure in the truck on the half-hour trip down to Whistlin' Jack Restaurant where she caught the bus. They sang silly songs; Katy shifted gears for him (she called it "driving") and learned to pour coffee from a heavy thermos while they moved down the narrow, snow-covered road. The bond between them was cemented in those dawn hours as they drove to the bus stop.

But nagging at my mind was the feeling that as she got older and her social needs became more sophisticated, she would resent the move to Goose Prairie. I, selfishly wanting this place and experience of the wilderness, feared I would lose her love and friendship. In that silent and lonely darkness I was, perhaps, transferring my own doubts and fears onto Katy. Those soothing, familiar voices of the radio announcers at NPR would bring me out of somber thoughts and provide comfort as I sat in the small circle of light at the kitchen counter waiting for daylight.

I realized, as I listened to the sunset and sunrise report, that in January during the darkest days, a minute was subtracted from the sunrise and a minute was added to the sunset. Adding the days we had left in January and multiplying that by two gave me an idea of when it would be light in the morning. I could tell Katy that by February first she would be able to see daylight as she got on the school bus at Whistlin' Jack and by the fifteenth of February she would be able to go down the hill to the car without using a flashlight. As the days got longer by a minute at a time on each end, my guilt about the move lessened as the promise of new light each day brightened the darkest corners of my thoughts.

Chapter Nineteen

PLUNGE TO THE DEPTHS

C inderella, Cinderella, la, la, la, it's Cinderella."

Katy, feather duster in hand, flitted around the apartment singing and humming parts of a song from the movie, *Cinderella.* She wore a small floral-print apron with lace on the sides, a dress, and tights. Very fitting for a girl acting as a servant.

"Mom, you have to be the wicked stepmother. Bear and Sam will be the stepsisters."

"Do I have to get up out of the chair to be the stepmother?" I was watching a movie with Tom while the generator was on for Saturday's "laundry evening."

"No, you just have to tell me to do things and you have to be mean." She made a face to show me what she meant by *mean.*

"Okay, I can be the stepmother. What about your father? Who's he going to be?"

"I don't know. Maybe the prince." Sometimes she was such a hoot.

"He always gets the good parts, Katy. Maybe he could be the stepmother."

"No," she shrieked. "He's a boy. He can't be the stepmother. You're the stepmother."

Apparently our roles were set. She began singing again, this time loudly.

"Cinderella," I said, "can you please do your cleaning quietly? The prince and I are trying to watch a movie." She giggled and continued to dust the furniture in the living area of the apartment.

Above was the small loft where we slept and behind us the ladder to get up there. A very low railing around the loft edge made me uneasy when I had to get up at night and descend the ladder. I made a mental note to ask Tom to raise the rail and add boards perpendicular to the floor to make it more secure. But I knew there were other things more urgent than a new rail. Next year will be soon enough, I thought.

I heard Katy humming her tune as bottles clinked and water splashed in the bathroom.

"What's going on in there?" I shouted over the noise.

"I'm doing the shower and the sinks now, wicked stepmother," was the response. "Should I mop the floors?"

"No, Cinderella. The shower and the sink will be enough. Why don't you clean around the steps? They're very dusty."

"I will as soon as I finish in here." The humming began again in earnest.

I went back to the movie. It was relaxing to be without guests on this long weekend. And no snow plowing until Monday afternoon since we didn't' have to go anywhere. Snow was still falling lightly. It was cozy in the apartment with the dogs, a fire in the fireplace, and the generator on. Tom was folding laundry and I put it away as Katy emerged from the bathroom with the duster.

She began with the bottom step of the ladder and swooshed the feathered wand front-to-back then side-to-side.

"Can we watch Cinderella when your movie is done?"

"Too late. By the time our movie is finished, you'll be going to bed."

"But it's not a school night."

"Right. But it's already nine o'clock and way past your bedtime. Make your way up the steps, Cinderella, and get your jammies on."

"Can I stay up until I finish cleaning the loft?" Any excuse to stretch the minutes until bedtime. "It's really dusty up here. What about fifteen more minutes?"

It was a Saturday night so why fuss with her? "Okay, fifteen minutes, but then it's right into bed. No whining."

"I won't." Humming and singing intermingled again as the duster was held high, then hugged like a dancing partner.

A huge pile of clean socks on the sofa awaited my attention. I began pairing the socks, separating them into piles for each of us. I could stuff them into the drawers when the movie was over. Tom sat down next to me and we concentrated on the movie's end.

Out of the corner of my eye, I saw Katy up above in the loft, stretching hard, trying to reach a corner of the rafters, which was beyond her reach. Before I could say anything, she lost her balance, slipped over the low railing and fell over the edge. On the way down, her face hit the pointed top of the laundry iron and her shoulder grazed the edge of the dresser on which the iron sat. There was nothing Tom or I could do to break her fall or catch her. She hit the floor behind the couch with a deadening thud.

"Oh, my gosh," I yelled as I ran to her. The tiny body was still. "Katy, Katy! Tom, she's not answering."

"Don't move her." He was quickly at my side. "Katy, honey, can you hear me?" Her eyes opened and she stared at her dad. "Katy, can you move your toes? Yes?" Katy was semi-conscious now. She began to cry.

"Can I pick her up, Tom?"

"Not yet. Katy, I'm going to move your legs and arms and you tell me if anything hurts too much." As he moved her limbs, she continued to sob. "Can you move your head from side to side for me, honey? That's fine. Rest for a minute." He sat back and sighed deeply.

"No broken bones that I can see." All that Scouting first aid was coming in handy. "But I think we need to take her to the hospital in case of a concussion or other head injury." Katy began to sob harder and louder at that statement. I put my arms all the way around her and hugged her.

"I don't want to go the hospital. I'm all right. I want to stay here. Please don't make me go. Please!" She was beginning to shiver. Tom got some blankets out of the closet and wrapped her in them.

"We have to make sure your head isn't injured, Kates. We'll stay with you." He was trying to explain without getting her more upset. He truly was a prince. "We'll get our coats on, wrap you up like an Eskimo baby and pull you down to the car on the sled. How about that?"

Through her tears she stared at her dad and then nodded. "Okay, Daddy."

"Right, Cinderella. You let Mom help you with your coat and boots and I'll go turn off the generator." He went out the back door, and, as I helped Katy with her winter clothes, the lights went out and the room was lit with the single gas lamp. I wrapped her again in the blanket and carried her upstairs to the front door. Tom brought the sled to the porch where we put her blanketed mummy-like figure onto the sled and quickly made our way down to the field below to the parked cars.

I put Katy in the front seat and sat in back behind her. She reclined the seat as we drove along the road.

"I'm tired now, Mama. I want to go to sleep."

Tom looked at me and shook his head.

"Sorry, babe," I said. "Maybe we can sing some songs or play a guessing game."

"But I'm so tired. I want to sleep." Her whiny voice was just a whisper.

"Katy, Dad says you can't go to sleep in case your head is injured. Please stay awake." I patted her gently on the cheeks and rolled her head gently so I could see her face. "Let's play "I Spy" even though it's dark. I spy something red."

Katy looked around and questioned me about several things in the car. We played the game until the lights of Yakima appeared in the distance. The hospital wasn't far from the freeway and I couldn't wait to get her there to have her under a doctor's care.

The waiting room was crowded. There were several children with runny noses and tear-laden eyes and adults with arms in make-shift slings, bandaged feet or legs. I told the receptionist our daughter had fallen about nine feet off a loft and been unconscious for a short time. Immediately she called a doctor and ushered us into an examining room. The doctor checked Katy's pulse, looked in her eyes, and felt her head. She was now wide awake and enjoyed the doctor's attention.

"Katy," the doctor said, "why don't you tell me how this happened." I started to answer for her but he put his finger to his lips and shook his head.

"I fell from our loft. I pretended I was Cinderella, but my foot slipped and that's all I remember. My cheek is sore. I think I hit something when I fell."

He put her face in his hand and felt her cheek lightly.

"Wow, you have a great big bump and it's getting red. Looks like you hit something with a point on it."

"I think she hit the iron on the way down," Tom said. "She was unconscious for a very short time."

The doctor looked at the two of us for a moment. "We're going to do some x-rays of her head and limbs just to be sure she's okay. Her eyes look normal but there's a large bump on her head. The nurse will be in to get her in a few minutes."

Fifteen minutes later a nurse arrived and asked Katy to get on the gurney. After reassurances from Tom, the nurse, and me that she would not be getting any shots, she hopped on.

As I stood to go with her, the nurse put her hand on my shoulder.

"No, we'll take her. We have a few questions we want to have her answer." She wheeled the gurney out of the room.

I was stunned. My daughter has a major accident and I can't be with her? I flopped back down onto the chair. Tom took my hand and squeezed it.

"She's a trooper and she'll entertain them all in there."

"The doctor thinks we hit her." I could feel the tears running down my cheeks. "I can't believe someone thinks we abuse our daughter." I thought I was going to be sick.

"It's the law, Kathleen. They have to check whenever a child comes in with injuries like this. They don't suspect us; they're just doing their jobs."

We sat in the examining room for what seemed like ages. Neither of us said a word. A model of the inner parts of the ear, disinfectant container labels, and boxes of plastic gloves provided a focal point of concentration as I tried to control my emotions.

The door suddenly flung open and Katy rode in on a wheelchair. It was a game to her now. The doctor helped her down. "We don't see anything abnormal. No swelling or broken bones. She will probably be achy and sore for the next couple days. Quiet activities for forty-eight hours. She's quite the talker and told us all about her accident. She sure is a happy girl for this time of night."

I looked at the doctor. There was no sign of accusation or judgment.

"Thank you for taking her so quickly," I said. "We came from Goose Prairie, an hour away."

"Oh, I know all about that. In fact, I know where you live, what you do, and how Katy gets to school each day. And, I'm sure if Katy spent more time here, I would know your whole life history!"

The doctor chuckled, shook Tom's hand, mine, and, finally, with exaggerated motion, Katy's. "You, Cinderella, are free to go home now."

The cold nighttime air felt wonderful on my face. I strapped Katy into the back seat, wrapped the blanket around her tightly, and planted a big kiss on the top of her head.

"I love you, sweetheart. I'm glad nothing's broken."

"Me, too, Mama. I'm going to sleep now. That doctor was nice." She was asleep before we got to the first traffic light.

"Is the lumberyard open on Sundays?" The railing was now my top priority.

"I was just thinking about that," Tom said. "That's my new weekend project."

Chapter Twenty

A GIFT FROM HOME

Spring arrived, not with the usual "in like a lion..." but with the lion standing beside the lamb. Cold rainy days followed a warm and sunny day or two, and then snow flurries and partly cloudy weather became the pattern for several weeks. The household fires didn't have to be fed as often, and by the beginning of April we lit a fire only on rainy days. I was relieved the wood in the shed had lasted throughout the cold season. Because the guest list wasn't as large as we had expected, the stacks of Douglas fir weren't depleted either.

Katy's grumpiness at being wrestled from bed each morning was now a tamer version of winter mornings. The light peeking through the apartment window at dawn as she got up helped to dissipate her bad mood. Katy's trek to the truck was now second nature, and a path to the parking area was clear of snow and ice. In the truck they made-up songs like "Alfalfa Hay" sung to the tune of "How Dry I Am," which helped pass the time on their way to the bus stop.

Katy had made friends with several other first grade girls on the bus. She liked the bus driver, Kirk, and looked forward to seeing him each morning when he greeted her with some witty comment meant to tickle the funny bone of a six-year old. She felt special since she was the first one on in the morning and the last one off in the late afternoon.

My daily routine lightened without the fire building and snow shoveling. In January I had finished my job at the church in Yakima in January and without that salary our expenses had exceeded our income for several months. The savings account had dwindled to nothing and the fear of unpaid bills was rekindled.

It was an in-between time in the forest. The weather continued to improve and hundreds of daffodils appeared under trees and in the fields around the house while wildflowers added their colorful hues to spring's bounty. But the ground was soggy and the weather still unpredictable. It was too late in the season to ski or go snowmobiling. It was too early to hike on the high mountain trails where snow was still falling and winter's damage to bridges and pathways made travel dangerous. We had a trickle of guests with no weekends entirely filled.

As a family we enjoyed the peace and quiet. Our first spring in Goose Prairie delighted us in the daily new ways Nature presented herself. We continued to wear our heavy winter boots because of the mud and unexpected piles of built up snow. But we no longer needed heavy coats, scarves, hats and thick woolen mittens. We had the forest and lake to ourselves.

One clear, warm Saturday in the middle of April, our family hiked across ice-packed snow to the edge of the lake where the last remnants of winter had melted under the sun's warm light. The sand beach was hot in comparison to the forest's shady space. We peeled off lightweight coats, sweaters, boots and socks, and played in the chilly water lapping gently on the shore. Samantha ran back and forth into the lake and up on the beach chasing whatever we could find to throw into the water. Bear stood close to the shore barking at Samantha's antics. We ate the picnic lunch thrown hastily into a backpack and took naps before putting our boots back on and heading over the snow toward home.

I liked sitting quietly on fallen trees or stumps to observe the activity of awakening animals. The elk were coming back up into the mountains from the lower elevations. Occasionally a deer hopped past or a porcupine lumbered by, and upon seeing me, made its way up the closest tree. Chipmunks scurried here and there and hawks and ravens flew overhead. The gusts of spring wind sang from the trees and just as suddenly, stopped. It was a celebration of new life I had never known before. As I sat, I pondered again what we were going to do about the ranch and its expenses.

I thought about going back to work in town but that would prevent me from increasing the Double K business. We had considered asking our families for another loan, but that would put us into more debt. Occasionally I preached at churches in the area and that brought in a little money, but not enough to sustain us until June when I hoped for more guests.

Late one Thursday afternoon at the end of April, I went to the bus stop to pick up Katy. I arrived early and stood in the telephone booth, which masqueraded as my office, and retrieved messages from our answering service in Yakima 60 miles away. There was a message from my mother to call her as well as some inquiries about the ranch. I returned the ranch calls keeping the response to my mother until last in the hopes the bus would arrive so Katy would have a chance to talk to her.

The bus was late. I dialed the number for Mom. She finally answered and we shared inconsequential things. I didn't like to bother her with the details of our problems. It induced needless worry on her part. I felt she had something on her mind and was building up to say it. When I sensed that over the phone, it usually meant she was angry about a sin of omission on my part. I ran through a mental list trying to think of what I might have forgotten, like a birthday, anniversary or other important date. I couldn't think of anything I'd missed so I listened patiently as she shared her concerns. It was getting chilly in the phone booth and I began to politely say goodbye.

"I have something I want to tell you." My mother suddenly sounded serious.

"What is it? It there something wrong?"

"No." There was a pause. "Your Aunt Helen left your dad a large sum of money. But I know that she would have wanted you and your sister Joann to have some of it as well. So, I am giving both you and your sister ten thousand dollars and you can do with it what you want."

I was stunned. Finally, I said, "Mom, you'll eventually need the money."

"No, I want you to have it. I know you can use it." She didn't know the half of it.

"Mom, this is a lifesaver. A ranch saver." My attempt at a feeble joke, but if I said one more word, I was going to cry.

"I'll send a check and then you'll have it."

We said our goodbyes and I stood inside the phone booth leaning heavily against the side. Who said money doesn't fall from heaven? My legs barely carried me out of the booth, and when Katy's bus arrived, I grabbed her out of the doorway and swung her to the ground with a huge hug and kiss.

"What's the matter, Mommy?"

"There's nothing the matter anymore, sweetheart. We are going to make it at the ranch!"

Katy was too young at six to understand the implications, but she was thrilled with my happiness and excitement. That she *could* understand.

I drove home in a euphoric state and couldn't wait to share the news with Tom. A miracle had occurred and we were right in the middle of it. With the bills paid and a little money in the bank, I could move on to the important job of creating a steady flow of guests.

Chapter Twenty-One

PERSISTENTLY BATTY

T he attic of the Double K Ranch had only two small windows at each end to provide light, but the ceiling, high and cathedral like, and the floor was a darkened pine. It was remote, peaceful and quiet. It provided storage space for holiday décorations, Tom's camping equipment, out of season clothing, and assorted memorabilia with which neither of us could bear to part. I kept my sewing materials in boxes in the attic so I was the one who went up there fairly often.

The first winter, my trips to the attic occurred only when the generator was operating. The windows provided very little daylight in the winter darkness and electricity allowed me to see the color of thread, the pattern of fabrics or the directions for a project. I also wanted to be sure goblins or other scary creatures weren't hanging out in the attic ready to get me. It took a few months before I was reasonably sure nothing out of the ordinary was happening up there.

One day toward the end of May of that first year, I climbed the stairs to the attic, walked around the chimney to the far end near the window and began opening boxes to search for fabric. It was light enough to see without a flashlight or the generated electricity. When I lifted a corner flap of one box, little bug size black pellets hit the floor and on closer inspection I realized they were mouse droppings. Piles of droppings were on some of the other boxes close to the windows but not on those further into the attic room. No mice seemed to be running around on the second floor so it was quite odd for them to be in the attic. I swept up the little piles and noticed more even closer to the windows. These droppings were all around the window frames and on the floor directly under the windows.

Ah, I thought. They are coming up through the walls by the windows or over the roof and climbing in under the sills. My knowledge of mice was limited to knowing that I didn't like them. They were sneaky and kind of messy in their habits. Knowing we had mice was okay. But it was disturbing not knowing how they got there and if there would be more. I went back downstairs to share the news with Tom.

"We've got mice in the attic. I found droppings close to the windows and on my boxes of fabric." He was reading the paper and hardly moved to acknowledge this catastrophe.

"Find any inside the boxes?"

"No, just on the tops and on the floor."

"Set some traps." Easy enough, I thought.

I put them around the boxes and close to the windows where the biggest piles of droppings were located. Every day I took great pleasure in going up to the attic and checking the traps for little mouse bodies. Day after day, more droppings, but no mice in the traps. I used cheese, peanut butter, popcorn and dog food to bait the traps, but each day they were empty, the droppings were mounting and the bait was still intact on the trap.

A powerful flashlight went with me on the next trip and I checked under the eaves and around the floorboards scouring each space for some sign of a mouse hole. Once again, nothing. I decided not to go to the attic for a few days so the mice would think I wasn't coming, get careless and trip the light fantastic over and into the traps.

A few days later, climbing the attic steps, I heard faint squeaking sounds. Tiptoeing around the chimney with my flashlight beam scanning the floor, I watched intently for any sign of movement. The squeaking stopped briefly and then started again. Quickly I moved my flashlight's beam towards the area the sound was coming from. There was nothing on the floor and nothing scurrying out of sight. I was stumped. The traps were empty and the bait still there. The squeaking sound was faint now and the direction of the sound was hard to discern. This was too creepy and taking up too much of my time, although the exercise up and down the steps several times a week was invigorating!

The mice I encountered in the basement were much more predictable. There might not be a dead mouse in a trap, but the bait would be gone and that meant a smart mouse, a defective trap, or too much bait, making it easy to get. If another trap was set, with smaller, more select bait, a mouse was dead in the trap the next day.

But up in the attic something else was happening. I was fixated on finding a solution to the problem. I went up with a better flashlight. Once again, I searched for tell tale signs of mice, trying to figure out how they got in and why I never saw one. There were no holes in the eaves, no trail of droppings showing me the way to the nest. I moved the flashlight slowly around shining it in every corner of each piece of wood hoping for a clue into this mouse mystery. As I got closer to the chimney, the squeaking became audible again. Coming around the corner, I stood quietly, planning each step in my mind, visualizing my next move like a cat ready to pounce on its prey. I turned the next corner and moved the beam of my flashlight quickly over the floor around the bricks, thinking that they were hiding between the boards and the bricks of the chimney. The beam caught a black blob lying quietly in the middle of the floor. It was directly under the highest part of the roof and it had some droppings around it. How strange. And then more squeaking. I was close; they had to be in the chimney. I squatted down and shined the light on the mouse. No tail, but it did have wings. It was clear and dreadful at the same time.

I pointed the flashlight upward and there, hanging from the boards in the very top of the attic roof, was a bunch of bats! There must have been a hundred fifty or two hundred of them, many with babies hanging from the fronts of their bodies. I was mortified. My bat knowledge consisted of ugly pictures, rabies deaths, and stories of bats tangling themselves in women's hair. I ran down the steps yelling for Tom. We met halfway up the stairs then climbed back up the steps together. I was breathless.

"What are we going to do? The guests will be frightened. What if the bats come in the *house*? Oh my gosh, what are we going to do?"

Tom shone the beam of light on the hanging bats up above. They became restless. I was afraid they would launch themselves from their perch, fly around and land on my head. Attack of the bats right here in my attic!

"Yep, those are bats. You'll have to find out what to do about them."

"Don't you know what to do?" He was a Scout. He was supposed to know everything about animals and their habitats.

"We have to seal the place up."

"What does that mean?"

"We have to find out where they are coming in and close the holes. But it's going to be hard because bats can fit through smaller holes than mice."

That evening at dusk, we went outside, positioning ourselves to see three sides of the lodge building. Sure enough, these little flying mice-like creatures came from the cracks around the windows and from underneath the roof. How were they getting between the wood and the metal roofing? Soon the sky was filled with bats, swooping down and quickly rising back up, and dipping downward again in an unpredictable flight pattern over our heads.

"They can eat six hundred bugs every night. They keep the mosquito population down, at least around our house." Were those words meant as comfort? The bats could eat a horse's weight in bugs. I didn't care. I just wanted them out of my attic.

Mice. If only it had been mice in the attic. Traps would have done the trick. I was trying to remain calm, but what if we couldn't get them out? What if we trapped them inside and they swarmed down into the house and tangled in our hair? What if they had rabies or worse, *what if they gave us rabies*? I had a lot to learn and I needed to do it fast. An exterminator seemed like the best bet. Mice, termites, rats, why not bats? Surely they could handle this problem.

Only one exterminator was willing to come up to Goose Prairie and "do" bats. He came several days later and we proceeded up the attic stairs to view what he called "the colony." He brought a bag with him and from that pulled out a huge flashlight.

"Whoa, good size group you got here." Group. That was somewhat more comforting than colony. The word colony, in re-lationship to bats, scared me. The pilgrims' had a colony and that grew into a country! I couldn't have that happening in my attic.

"I think you got yourself a nursery colony. Babies hanging off their mothers. Colony's gonna grow." Just what we needed, a nursery here in the attic. Not only did I have to contem-plate kicking bats out of my house, I was evicting mothers and babies as well.

"What do we do then?" Meaning what was *he* going to do.

"Well, there are a couple of things we can do. When we find out where they are going in and out, we can put bags with blades over the openings. Then when they fly out they'll get killed in the bag."

Oh, my. My stomach shuttered and turned. I couldn't stand the thought of carved up bats in bags hanging from the third floor of the lodge. And what would I tell the guests when they asked? Oh, they are just directional windbags like you see on some bridges affected by wind velocity. No, that was not going to happen in my attic.

"What else?" Surely there was a better solution.

"We can poison them by putting a powder on the boards around the colony and then they'll die. Hopefully while they are out getting water. Kind of like rat poison."

The old poison route.

"What happens to them then?"

"You have to pick 'em up. I saw you've got dogs. It wouldn't be good for the dogs, because they'd pick them up and eat them or carry them around. Kill the dogs, too, soon enough. Or make them real sick." This method was not an option.

"Any other possibility for just getting rid of them, not destroying them?" Killing them off seemed so barbaric, especially since we were in their forest. But I wanted them out of the attic.

"Don't think so. They are pretty persistent about coming back to the same place. But you could try filling the holes where you think they're coming in."

I thanked him for coming and said I would be in touch. Those methods seemed too messy and uncivilized. Even though I wanted them out, savagery wasn't my thing. Not for a bunch of moms and their babies.

I studied up on bats myself realizing that asking exterminators to help keep things alive was an oxymoron. After my research, and with a nod towards environmental sanity and humanity, I called the Forest Service.

The ranger came out to the ranch the next day. Hearing a tone of desperation in my voice, he wanted to be sure that nothing happened to the bats before he could study them. He acted as if Mother Earth had come upon the lodge and, just as the stork leaves babies, had left us bats. My lack of thankfulness that these creatures had flown forth and attached themselves to our attic boards baffled him.

"You are so fortunate. And a nursery colony, at that. Bats are really good creatures with a bad reputation. We can study this colony close up if you'd like. You could build a bat box and hang it from one of your trees about a hundred yards from the house.

Put guano all over it and maybe they'll move to it." Okay, this was move positive and less messy than the exterminator.

"How long 'til they move out if I put up a bat box?"

"No telling. Sometimes they move and sometimes they don't. If they like it up here maybe never." How reassuring. "These bats migrate, that's why they are only here in the summer. Winter is too cold and with the snow on the roof I'm sure it's way too cold for them to stay. After they leave you can fill up the holes where you think they're getting in. See if that helps."

This proposal had a lengthier time frame than I had planned, but was far more merciful than poison or bags of bat parts flapping in the breeze from the third story of the lodge.

On August twentieth, there was no sign of the bats. They left piles of guano (good for plant fertilizer, bad to breathe), but at least they were gone. We could now figure out how to keep them out permanently.

We spent September looking around the attic, not only at the floor area, but also all along the eaves and roof. In one section of the roof, which was behind the chimney and unlit by both the generator lighting and natural light, there was fire damage that hadn't been repaired properly. A metal roof had been laid over the top of the burned wood. The damage was quite extensive and provided an opening for the bats to make their migratory trip into the attic each season, and their nocturnal meal flight each evening.

The Forest Service gave us a bat box, which we hung in a dead tree. We got started on closing up the holes, filling them with yellowish, frothing foam insulation, putting it in every crevice and space from the window frame to the roof. It was like painting with aerosol string only when the foam came out of the can it blew up to five times its original size. Our beautiful attic was now a psychedelic art piece worthy of its fifteen minutes of fame. The nature of our success or failure in this endeavor would come to light in May.

On May twentieth of the next year, I climbed the attic stairs holding a large flashlight, walked around the chimney and shone the beam up to the site of the "bat motel." No bats! Could it be true? Had we managed to fill all the holes and keep them out? I was thrilled but cautiously skeptical.

In the attic the next day, I shone the beam up into the roof eaves and saw two, tiny black bodies. I could deal with two as long as they weren't using the attic as an incubator for increasing the bat population. My heart was filled with glee going down the steps to report to Tom. He didn't say anything, but his raised eyebrows and tilted head expressed a "wait and see" attitude.

I did not have to *wait* long to *see*. The rest of the group returned the next day and began their work expanding the colony through birth. The bats "squatting" in our attic was discourteous at best, but the panic I felt at their return was minute compared to the previous summer. Through the research I had done over the previous year, I had learned what was truth and what was myth. Perhaps there was even a little interest in them developing!

The bat colony became less of a concern until one summer night. I was asleep in the loft with Tom and Katy and we didn't have guests that evening. I woke to hear a strange sound.. A shadow moved around the kitchen and I couldn't figure out what it was. I got down from the loft and as I did a bat flew into the apartment fluttering around the bed, circling and then swooping down towards me. I yelled for Tom, who was still asleep and he saw it as he woke.

"Open all the doors! Get a broom!"

The shadows the bat was creating with its erratic movement were grotesque especially at 2 a.m. It appeared far bigger to me than I knew it was. I wanted it out. How many more were flying around in the house? I ran up to the second floor and shut the attic door to prevent any more bats from flying through the house. Tom chased the bat with the broom until it flew out the door into the cool night air. So much energy for such a small creature!

The bats stayed the summer and left on schedule. Their presence was not agreeable to me for the most part, but I must give them credit. They arrived promptly when expected and did not overstay their visit.

The bats' habits never changed. For three more years, we added foam to the "attic art" and every year they found a way into the nursery high above. If I'm ever on a game show and they ask me to provide a question for the answer "persistent," I will respond with "What is a bat's most conspicuous characteristic?"

Chapter Twenty-Two

THE ANTS COME MARCHING.

Early in June Tom left for ten days to direct a Boy Scout training program near Seattle. Katy and I enjoyed being at the ranch by ourselves without a schedule of school and guests. I had no other appointments except to preach for a little church on the outskirts of Yakima.

On Sunday, we put the dogs in, locked the house, and drove to town. The weather was hot and sunny with hardly a breeze in the air. It had been this way for a few days and we agreed summer had finally arrived in full regalia. The cheerful wildflowers along the roadside and the blooms in gardens throughout town proclaimed summer's arrival too.

After the church service, Katy and I drove home. As we approached the lodge, Katy wanted to lean out the car window. I agreed she could do it while we rounded the end of the house and drove slowly along the backside of the building. Pulling to a stop, I heard Katy say something in a low voice spoken with a mixture of fear and awe.

"What did you say, honey?" I turned the noisy car off and it was quiet.

"Oh my gosh." This time I heard her.

"Has the house been broken into? What's wrong?"

I got out of the car and looked at the building. No broken windows and the back door was intact. But covering the whole backside of the house were thousands, if not millions, of ants. Big black ants with bulbous heads and equally large bodies. Some had wings and were flying in mad patterns around the other ants on the house and ground. Others crawled in and out of the seams of the wooden shingles. They looked like carpenter ants, but they had wings. Oh, my gosh, I thought.

"Get in the car, Katy. We have to go to the hardware store in town." She climbed in immediately and didn't complain about going back to town. I drove fast. If those *were* carpenter ants I knew they might eat through the house before we got back.

At the hardware store, I described the ants to the salesman. He looked very concerned, showed me some products, which were safe for animals on the ground, and I purchased them all. I left the store with $140.00 worth of sprays, powders, and granules and the salesman's assurance that these would take care of the problem.

Once home, I sprayed the wooden shingles on the outside of the house and laid down the powder and granules five feet out from the foundation. Immediately the black ant motion on the house seemed less, either from the insecticide or my wishful thinking.

Inside the house I found a few ants in the great room and none in the dining room. I checked the bedrooms upstairs in the lodge and they seemed clear of activity. The dogs, usually bothered by flying insects or bugs crawling along the ground, seemed unconcerned when they sniffed around outside.

Katy and I went to bed that night with some trepidation about ants dropping on us or keeping us company in the beds, but our apartment seemed clear of bugs. The next morning I went out the back door to check on the effectiveness of my expensive lot of insecticides. Tons of dead ants lay around the foundation. But the feeling of victory was short-lived. As the day warmed, ants began to congregate on the wooden shingles; soon they were flying and crawling all around the building.

Toward evening, with the air still and the sun low over the far ridge, the ants came marching, two-by-two, four-by-four, eight-by-eight and more, until the surfaces outside were covered once again.

Katy and I retreated into the apartment where we felt safe from the invasion. After a late dinner, I tucked her into her bed.

"Can you leave the gaslight on, Mommy?"

"Of course, sweetheart. You'll be fine. I haven't seen more than one or two ants in here since yesterday." She was worried, but trying to be brave about the crawling creatures. I was concerned, but tried to sound nonchalant.

Then I went to bed in the loft. The bed was close to the ceiling because of the pitch of the roof, but we didn't mind since it was tongue and groove wood and had a cozy feel. The space was warm, especially since I had left the gaslight burning. As I lay there, I thought I saw some movement overhead. Silly, I thought. Just my imagination. But, I watched the ceiling. A black bulbous head appeared from between the grooves and dropped onto the bed. I stifled a scream and scrambled from the bed. Looking up again, I saw there were now several ants crawling along the grooves, occasionally dropping to the bed or the floor. This was truly disgusting and my first reaction was to grab Katy, get dressed and go to town for the night, but I knew that was impractical and a waste of money. I had to come up with a better solution.

I went downstairs and grabbed a roll of masking tape. Back up in the loft, I began the laborious task of putting tape over all the grooves. When I had finished, masking tapes ran in stripes along the ceiling from the head of the bed to the ceiling and from the foot of the bed where the roof was pitched the highest. That seemed to solve the problem, at least for the moment. If the ants got any worse, Katy and I would have to move to the bedrooms in the main part of the house.

When Katy got up in the morning, she wanted to know what the tape was for. I told her I was taking precautions and putting tape up in case ants came into the loft bedrooms. Because she was six, my explanation seemed to satisfy her curiosity.

That evening I again put her to bed, assuring her that all was well and that I would leave the light on again. She fussed a little and then finally seemed to settle down for the night. I was reading a book in our apartment's little living room when I heard her call out.

"Mommy, can you come up here?"

"Katy, you need to go to sleep."

"Mommy, I need you to come up here."

"I'm not coming up, Katy, and you need to go to sleep."

I could hear a little sniffling going on, but knew, from other nights, this was her bedtime routine.

"*Mommy.*"

"Katy, I'm not going to be pleased if I come up there and nothing is wrong."

"*Please* come up, Mommy."

I went up the loft ladder mumbling, "this better be good!" Rounding the guardrail I looked over at her bed, and, saw what seemed like hundreds of ants crawling up the wall and across the ceiling. Katy was huddled in a little ball under her sheets trying to shield herself from the ones dropping onto her bed. I grabbed her, hugged her tight and helped her go down the ladder, apologizing profusely as we went. Ah, I thought, another layer of guilt for me to deal with later in life.

As suddenly as they had appeared, they disappeared. Every once in a while I would see one in the forest or near the foundation of the house, but not flying or in the house. For ten days it had been like the Biblical plague of locusts, and we had survived.

Embarrassment played a role in my inability to talk to some of the other Goose Prairie residents about this. What would they think about the ants? In all the years I had been coming to Goose Prairie, no one had ever mentioned ants. A day or two after they disappeared, my anxiety about the situation spilled out over coffee at the Goose Prairie Inn.

"Denny, have you ever had ants? The big, black carpenter ants?"

"Yeah. Just had 'em all last week."

"You had them too? I thought I was the only one."

"Nope. They come out every year after the first three or four days of hot, dry weather, then a week or two later, they're gone."

"*Every year?*"

"Every year."

"Where do they come from? There were thousands of them on the outside and by the end, they were all over the apartment. Then they just disappeared. Weird."

"All the old wood in the forest. Sometimes they stay for a short time, sometimes they stay longer," he commented as he finished cleaning up the counter and went back into the kitchen carrying a few dishes and coffee cups. I drank my tea, contemplated what he told me, and left some money by the cash register as I called goodbye.

When I was in town the next day, I bought some books on ants and their habits and habitats. I read that a person has to find the main nest and all of its satellite nests and destroy them. The best way to do that was to follow the ants at midnight using a flashlight as they returned to the nests; it is there you must eradicate them.

I shared this theory of ant hunting with Tom when he returned home.

"Very practical, Kathleen, *especially* in the forest. How much rotten wood *can* you cover in a lifetime? How many nests and satellites do you think are in a forest?"

Thinking about it that way made me laugh out loud. "That's one of the reasons I married you, Tom. Perspective."

"Live with it. It's temporary and it has been going on long before this house was built and for the forty years after, and notice, the house is still standing."

"I know, but they're so awful and creepy, peering out from the cracks and falling from the ceiling."

"Yeah, but with all the chemicals you're spraying, we'll either be dead of cancer or bankrupt before they consume the house."

"Ha, funny boy." I sat in silence, knowing that he was right. There was no damage to the house or the inspector would have found it. There was plenty of wood for them to eat in the forest and our house was a dried out forty-year-old morsel. But the thought of the ants coming unannounced next year, and every year after, crawling on the beams, dropping onto the furniture, marching across the back of the sofa, was almost unbearable. Perhaps next year would be less stressful. This year I had envisioned them as permanent guests. Now I knew their visit was short-lived.

"Okay. I'll just spray the outside of the house next year and spray inside when I see one. We'll buy a dozen fly swatters and have them around in every room."

"Cheaper and safer."

Tom was done with the conversation and the ants for this year. I tucked the experience away but the creepy feeling only lessened and never fully subsided.

Chapter Twenty-Three

GUESTS AND GAS LAMPS

P amco representatives knocked on our door one balmy summer afternoon in late July. The construction company, beginning work on the Bumping River dam in September, was looking for housing for the crew. Someone at the Goose Prairie Inn had suggested we might be willing to house the workers during fall, winter and spring.

I showed them around the lodge pointing out amenities: a generator providing electricity in the evenings, a coal furnace, and regular meal service would make their stay more comfortable. They wanted to know if I would prepare all three meals, and pack lunches each day for the men to eat at the worksite. Assuring them I was willing to accommodate them in this respect, I also shared that we didn't allow smoking, the weekends needed to be free for other guests, and I had a young impressionable daughter so excessive drinking was out as well.

Tom, the supervisor, spoke up.

"The men we want to house are family men. I'm sure they will respect your concerns. What would the price be?"

I quoted our standard rate. It was already so low that I didn't offer them a special price for staying so long. I could see them looking at each other with a degree of surprise.

"How many people would be interested in staying if you decide this is the right place?"

"We've got about eight to twelve guys who would stay regularly. Two or three will need a place when they are doing specialty work for us at the dam." My brain's agile cash register was doing a quick estimate of each week's gross income. This could be a bonanza.

"We can house up to sixteen," I replied.

"I think each man needs his own room to call 'home.' They're working alongside each other all day and need some breathing room at night."

"Then ten comfortably. Can the specialty people share rooms?" I wanted to appear as accommodating as possible. We needed this business. It would make the coming winter easier and our financial burden much lighter.

"Sure. That would work. Those men would only be here a few days at a time. The only concern I have is with the lighting. The mornings are going to be dark in winter and the men will need to be at work at dawn. Can you run the generator in the morning as well?"

I thought for a few moments. We kept a log of the number of hours we used the generator. This allowed us to regulate fuel usage since we couldn't get the tank filled between late October and early May. I had no idea how much fuel would be used running it an extra hour each day all winter long.

"I'm not sure we can because there's no fuel delivery in the winter."

"We might be able to get up there with our trucks. What do you think, guys?"

The suggestion wasn't met with overwhelming affirmation. I hoped this wouldn't dissuade them from staying at the lodge.

"My husband Tom and I have been talking about installing propane gas lamps on the first floor. If we knew you were going to stay, we could go ahead with that." Nothing like making a commitment without discussing it with Tom first.

They looked at each other in silent consensus. After discussing how payment would take place, a tentative schedule of work and meals, and where the men would park their trucks, they left giving me a "possible maybe" on the way out the door.

It was several weeks before we heard from Pamco. The guest book had been filling steadily for future weekends. Most reservations were for Friday evening through Sunday noon, which would give me a chance to get the lodge turned around before the work crew returned on Monday evenings.

I was anxious for the gaslights to go in and knew it would take a few weeks once we contracted with the propane company. Every day I checked messages from my phone booth "office". I had started to count on this and if it didn't I was going to be very disappointed.

The call finally came from Pamco. The men would be staying from mid-September until sometime in the spring. Six would be staying with us, while the others, described as "liking their cigarettes and drink," would stay in a rented cabin closer to the lake. Pamco explained that a couple men might change their minds and stay with us after giving the house a try for a week or two. Six steady guests each week for three seasons, supplemented by weekend guests, would provide the business for which we had been hoping. But, it was being provided in an unexpected way!

The propane contractors arrived soon after and began installing the lamps, two on each support beam in the great room, four in the dining room, one at the desk and bottom of the steps and two new lights in the kitchen.

Initially, I had some concern about the pipes filled with propane running the full length of the basement under the house. I knew gas was highly flammable and could explode. The furnace was a potential problem in winter. But the workmen assured me the pipes were far enough away from it and that rarely was propane a problem.

In mid-August, after the workmen had finished and darkness began to close in on us one evening, we lit the lamps. Just a turn of the knob to start the gas, a flick of the lighter, and presto there was light. After a year of darkness in the evenings, except on those special occasions when we used the generator, this was spectacular. During our first year at the Double K, we had used kerosene lanterns from Lehman's, the Amish store in Ohio or we'd huddled under a single gaslight in our apartment. It became routine for us to go to bed as soon as the natural light of day was gone. Now, no one had to turn on the generator, fill the kerosene lamps, trim wicks, change the filament shade, breath the black smoke or worry about the fire danger of open-flamed lamps. And, no one had to jockey for the best position under the lamp in the apartment. We had light, a new source of income and life was looking up.

Chapter Twenty-Four

SETTLING IN

Katy was very excited about starting school the second year. She had friends, knew the bus routine, liked the driver and now, she was going to have playmates at the ranch for the whole school year. That's how *she* envisioned the role of the Pamco workers. She asked me if I thought they would want to color, play games or read to her. I responded that they were not staying with us for her enjoyment, but rather because they had a job to do at the dam. She was skeptical of my explanation and eagerly awaited their arrival to set things straight.

During the second week of September, late one Monday afternoon, the Pamco crew arrived. They dropped off their bags and left to inspect the worksite. My stomach was a bit fluttery when I met them. I realized they would be staying a long time. What if we didn't hit it off? What if they were rude and swore or were impolite to my family? As usual, my mind was racing off to the "what ifs" instead of staying in the present and assessing the situations as they occurred. Perhaps there wouldn't be any major problems.

I drove to the bus stop at Whistlin' Jack and while I waited for Katy to arrive, I went in the store and picked up milk, eggs and a few other last minute items. I wanted to be thoroughly prepared to make Pamco's first week at the ranch as perfect as possible. And then it occurred to me what the nervousness was about. It wasn't about how the men would act. It was about their feelings toward me and the accommodations we were providing. What if they didn't like my cooking, or the bedrooms, or the lodge itself? What if they decided to move out within a week? I was depending on this income.

My traumatic thought pattern was broken by the sound of the bus braking in front of the store. After paying for my groceries, I went outside and called to Katy who was climbing down the steps of the bus. She ran over and gave me a hug while still calling goodbyes to Kirk, the bus driver.

"Good day at school?" I noticed that her bangs seemed stiff and stuck way out and up from her forehead.

"We had a great time on the bus. Rachel and Emily brought some curlers and hairspray and we did our hair on the way to school. And, we didn't have to sit in our assigned seats today. If we're good on the trip we don't have to all week."

"Wonderful, but how was school?"

"Okay. I've got to use the rest room before we go home."

Katy arrived back at the car and we drove toward the ranch.

"I have a surprise for you when we get home, Kates."

"Tell me now. I want to know now."

"Nope. You'll see when we get home. You'll like the surprise."

Pamco trucks were parked on the far side of the driveway when we drove up the lane. Katy squealed with excitement and gave my arm a big squeeze. As soon as the car stopped she opened the door, leapt out and headed for the back door. I grabbed the groceries and followed. The men were seated inside around one dining room table. Katy, who had been all energy, stopped at the kitchen counter.

"And who is this we have?" One of the men turned and gave her a wink. She smiled and moved toward them.

"I'm Katy. I live here." She moved closer and looked them all over one by one.

"You are going to stay with us. Do you like to play games?"

They all laughed and any tension about introductions and how this would all work out dissolved.

I took them upstairs to their rooms, showed them the two bathrooms and discussed the arrangements for meals. Dinner would be at six each night and breakfast at six in the morning. I would have the lunches ready to go after breakfast. I discussed what they liked and what they didn't, and tried to get a feel for the kinds of meals they were expecting. They assured me they would eat just about anything. We agreed that if they didn't like something I fixed they would tell me so I wouldn't prepare it again.

Dinner that night was fun. Some of the men were more talkative than others, but they liked joking around and seemed to enjoy the atmosphere. When dinner was finished, they went into the great room, did some reading, and by eight p.m. they had all gone upstairs. The lodge was quiet.

The next morning I got up at five, went into the kitchen, began making coffee for all the thermoses, stuffed sandwiches, fruit, chips, and cookies into paper bags and broke eggs in preparation for breakfast. Soon I heard water running upstairs and the sounds of groaning at the early hour, as the men got ready for work. They came down right at six and except for a few "good mornings" and "pass the butter," didn't say much.

Katy came up from the apartment all dressed for school. I was amazed since I usually had to cajole her out of bed and into her clothing. She took her seat at the table and joined in at breakfast like one of the workmen. They made room for her as if this were normal procedure. All my "what ifs" were laid to rest that morning. These were nice men, polite, caring, and respectful of our place and family. This was going to be fun. An adventure in living!

Weeks passed in which a routine was established. The men began each day in near silence, ate quickly and were out the door with their lunches before six-thirty. They came home at night filled with stories of the workday, read in the living room and then one by one went upstairs to bed. Each night someone was willing to read to Katy or play games like dominoes, "War" or "Sorry". By mid-November each person who sat at the table in the great room had one of her coloring books and when I looked in after finishing the dishes, two or three men were bent over, crayon in hand, intently coloring the latest "Mickey Mouse" or "101 Dalmatians" illustration.

The Double K Ranch was finally a "real" business. I had guests all week and again on most weekends. Monday night we'd be back to the routine. It was a healthy rhythm that infused my life. I was busy, content and, most importantly, providing another income for our family.

I enjoyed having people around who had the skills and talents I lacked. These men could fix the generator if necessary, fiddle with the gas lamps if there were a problem and with winter closing in, had the equipment to plow the driveway on their way out each morning and on their way in every night.

Katy loved knowing that people were at the ranch almost all the time and her days and evenings sailed by with hardly a whine or complaint, a welcome change from the previous year. Tom didn't express many feelings about Pamco being with us, but I could tell he was pleased because Katy and I were satisfied with the situation and neither of us complained to him about much of anything. He could relax a little, too, and not worry about our finances, which made him happiest of all.

Chapter Twenty-Five

TREES, TREATS AND GOODWILL TO ALL

December arrived quickly that year. Most of the first week was spent decorating each picture window with garlands, miniature musical instruments, and large cardboard angels holding trumpets, which I had cut out and sprayed-painted red, green and gold. Over the fireplace hung an angel I saw at a Yakima fabric store and re-created at home. Golden, curly hair surrounded her cherubic features, her dress was made of draped velvet, and she held a small version of a trumpet I'd found in a local flea market. Tom hung her from the fireplace with fishing line and she magically "flew" across the front of the massive rock fireplace, her bare feet peeking out from the edge of her velvet dress.

I wanted a pine or spruce from the forest for our Christmas tree. We had high ceilings and lots of space as well as many interesting ornaments we hadn't been able to hang in past years because our tree was too small. Tom didn't mind going into the forest to cut a tree, but the idea of hauling it back to the house wasn't his idea of fun. We had lots of trees on our land and decided to cut one of those instead.

Tom, Katy, and I bundled up late one afternoon when Tom got home from work. We trudged around the property, the dogs following closely behind. It was cold and felt like it would rain soon. We circled the property and came back near the front of the house.

"How about this one?" Tom pointed to one that was near the driveway. "It looks fairly straight. Not too big."

"No, I don't think it's big enough for the living room. I want it to look majestic in there. How about this one?" I pointed to a very tall, wide spruce.

"Too big and wide. We'd hardly be able to get it through the front door."

We walked a little further and he pointed to another one. I shook my head.

"No, not that one either. Can't you see the bare spot on the other side?"

"We'll put it up against a wall. No one will see it."

"I don't want the tree up against the wall. I want people to walk around it and see all the decorations."

It was getting dark and starting to drizzle.

"You're not going to get the perfect tree." Tom was getting impatient with the looking. He wanted to cut one down, get it into the house before it was drenched, and begin decorating. Katy and the dogs had already headed back to the house.

"How about we get the one I liked up near the house?" I needed to break this impasse. "I like the shape of it and it doesn't have any bare spots that I can see. Let's get that tree."

"It's too big and the needles are too sharp. You're not going to like decorating it." Tom's voice held a tone of irritation.

"But it's the closest one to perfect we've found and I like it." It was raining harder. I saw Tom shrug his shoulders and grab the saw.

"Okay, but no complaints when we get it in the house."

"No complaints. I promise."

The tree fell to the ground a minute later. We grabbed the trunk and a few of the lower branches and dragged it back to the house. It certainly looked bigger now that it was on the ground. And the needles were poking through my mittens like big brambles on a blackberry bush. Perhaps Tom had been right. I wouldn't admit that and I wouldn't complain. I had made my promise.

In order to get the tree through the door, Tom pulled and I pushed. The needle pricks now felt like razors cutting across my hands as I pushed against them to get the tree moving. With one great heave-ho, the tree went through the door and landed on the wooden floor, covering it with water and dead debris from the tree itself and other forest plants. Tom cut off some of the branches close to the bottom and shoved the tree into the metal tree holder.

"Let's stand it up, Tom. I can't wait to see what it's going to look like in here."

He pushed the bottom toward me and I pushed the top toward him. He stopped.

"Wait! He leaned over and looked at the base of the tree. "It's too big and I'm going to have to cut a whole lot off the bottom to make it fit in here." I lowered the tree to the floor. Tom took the tree out of the holder, got the saw, and cut a foot off the bottom. We pushed and pulled again until it was almost upright, but it was still too tall. He looked at me with "I told you so" darting from his eyes as we laid it down and went through the same process again. If he had to trim much more, it was going to lose its shape. Again, we pushed and pulled it until it stood up, its top branches skimming the ceiling.

"Hold the tree there until I get some cord to anchor it to one of the posts and the wall." He walked out of the great room.

Not only was this tree tall, it was wide. It took up a whole corner in the great room and although the space was very large, the tree dwarfed it. The needles poked me in my side and arm and, when I wasn't careful, my face. I hopped from one foot to the other trying to get more comfortable while wishing my arms were about a foot longer. How long was it going to take Tom to get the cord? He was probably sitting in the workshop laughing about me holding this prickly, too big, tree and taking his time coming back.

But he re-appeared shortly and we got the tree tied up. I stepped back from it, way back, and gave a good, hard look. It was a fair looking tree. Not as spectacular as it had been outside, not quite majestic, but good. And big.

"Maybe we could leave it undecorated this year?" I was sure my arms were pocked marked under my sleeves from the needles.

"I don't think so. The reason you wanted a big tree was to put all the ornaments on it, so let's get busy and get it done."

Tom began opening all the boxes we had carried down from the attic and handed me the ornaments one by one. Katy joined in, but soon complained about the needles and decided instead, to entertain us with her violin playing and a solo rendition of the songs her music class was singing at the school program.

When we finished, the tree was more beautiful than I had imagined it could be. Tiny instruments, homemade dough ornaments, Santa faces, religious symbols and a variety of glass ornaments in different shapes and textures all had space to hang gracefully and show themselves off. A painful process, I thought, but well worth it.

The Pamco crew left at the end of the third week of December and wasn't returning until the New Year. Tom insisted that the few days before and after Christmas be set-aside for family and friends without guests. We had always gone to Tom's parents' house for Christmas, but when we moved to Goose Prairie we were no longer able to do that. We had to keep the "the home fires burning". Literally. So did most of the other people on the Prairie and had family come to them instead of going away. That meant children for Katy to play with and several impromptu social gatherings with neighbors. We enjoyed morning coffee accompanied by rich, buttery pastries, afternoon hot chocolate with a "nip" added, or wine and cheese in the evening. Whoever was around joined in the fun.

On Christmas Eve, Katy, with Tom's encouragement, left cheese and crackers rather than cookies and milk for Santa. She made a tape for Santa to listen to as he munched on the goodies. It was filled with songs from her program at school, her list of the good work she had done both in school and at the Goose Prairie Inn, and her thanks for what she seemed sure was in store for her the next morning. She also told Santa he was too big for the fireplace in our apartment and since it had an insert, he couldn't use that route anyway. With all that important communication taken care of, we tucked her into bed, made sure she was asleep, and brought out the gifts spreading them under the plentiful boughs of the Christmas tree.

A light dusting of new snow on the old coal-stained drifts, the lights of the too-big, but almost perfect tree, the decorations at each window and the gifts lying in wait for a little girl's anxious touch, made the evening a memorable one and seemed to sum up all that I hoped the ranch would be to our family and to our guests: a place of spiritual warmth, generosity and most of all, fun.

The day after Christmas, our friends, Barb and Cragg Gilbert, along with their sons Nathaniel and Sean came to stay for a couple of days. They had been our biggest fans and supporters throughout the trials of getting the ranch and in the difficult first year of living there. I had known the Gilberts since our time together in seminary at Princeton. Tom and Cragg hit it off when they met each other for the first time, both dedicated advocates of single-malt whiskies. The Gilberts came bearing gifts of bacon, pasta, cheeses, breads and their two sons, whom Katy had known since birth.

Nathaniel and Sean, ages thirteen and ten, along with seven-year-old Katy, immediately headed outside for the hill behind the house and began developing a "daring"(as they called it) sled run. It was an architectural project as well as an engineering feat and the fine art of negotiation was practiced as the development of the run needed to please two growing boys and one little girl.

They planned two routes, an easy one that went straight down into a snowdrift, and a hard one, that ran down a hill, up a ramp, over a very large tree stump, and ended in a sharp turn to miss the right hand corner of the garage. The garage was the final destination, one way or another. Success in the run put the rider in the garage. Failure meant being plastered to the outside wall with snow as the only cushion.

The children amused themselves for hours on the sled runs, trying different sleds, body positions and stances. After watching them for a while, and joking about who would take the children to the hospital with broken legs and arms, we parents went back inside and sat around the blazing fire in the living room, each choosing a favorite chair, near the fire or away, depending on personal need for warmth at the moment. Every so often we switched seats, adjusting our distance rather than dampening the fire in any way.

Barb and I chatted about things going on in town, while Cragg and Tom caught up with business, Scouting, and world issues in general. We drank coffee by the pot and sipped tea like the British. At dusk, we loaded up trays with appetizers, soft drinks and hot chocolate, brought out the bottle of single malt whiskey Cragg wanted Tom to try, and called the children to come inside.

In a few minutes, soaking wet clothes sizzled on the coal furnace grate and the children's painfully red hands, feet and faces moved close to the fireplace. Katy sat in her little rocker and the boys threw themselves into overstuffed chairs facing the fire. Periods of silence, tidbits of conversation and a deep contentment with life in general (specifically with our own lives) filled the room as the heat of the fire and the warmth of the Scotch permeated our bodies.

Dinner was a haphazard feast. Ham, salads, cheeses, bread and whatever else we found in the refrigerator or outside the back door tucked in the snowdrift (a makeshift icebox) were put on the table. We ate amidst laughter, silly antics, and great stories of Christmases gone by. Soon the children asked to be excused. Renewed by the food, warmed by the fire and rested by short naps in the great room, the children played board games, put puzzles together, and tried their hand at cards. Soon, Nathaniel, the oldest child, was the only one awake enough to walk up to his room. We all followed shortly carrying the younger ones to their beds.

What better Christmas could I ask for? The solitude of the mountains, soft light from the gas lamps, the fingers of the fire's warmth spreading throughout the room, and the company of best friends was all the peace and goodwill we needed to move us into a new year.

Chapter Twenty-Six

THE PLAN

During January and February the temperature dropped to fourteen degrees for one or two nights but stayed at or near freezing the rest of the time. This moderate climate made working at the dam much easier than the crew expected so they were ahead of schedule on the project. They would probably be leaving the ranch a few weeks earlier than anticipated.

We continued to enjoy their company and their help. One night they came in laughing and hooting like I'd not heard before. Craig, an easy going, quiet fellow, who worked in the water, had put on a wetsuit that morning and after getting himself into it realized there was a mouse in one foot. The mouse ran up his leg and then back down, going nowhere because the suit was tight. He struggled to get it off but was not initially successful. Everyone else was laughing so hard they couldn't help him take it off. It was the story of the day and carried over into the night.

One evening I went to turn off the generator after our family movie. I walked down to the garage, flicked the generator switch and turned to go, expecting it to shut down as usual. Instead, it kept operating and gasoline began spewing all over the floor and the other generator. I flipped the switch several more times, but nothing happened. I ran back to the house and called for Tom. He came down with me and tried the same things I had.

"Let's get Craig." The fuel spilling all over the garage scared me. "I know he's asleep, but he won't mind. "

"You go get him," Tom said, still trying to stop the flow.

"I can't go in his room. I'll be too embarrassed. He'll be embarrassed. You go."

He left without saying a word and I continued to watch the generator.

Tom and Craig returned shortly. Craig took one look at the liquid shooting from the machine and shoved his hand over the air intake valve. The sucking sound on his palm was intense. In a few seconds, the diesel fuel stopped squirting. The generator sputtered and shut down.

We apologized for getting him out of bed and asked about his hand.

"It's fine. This is not unusual for these generators and I'm glad you thought to wake me. That's what we're here for."

That night I gave a mighty thank-you to the God of the universe both for Craig's knowledge and kindness and for Pamco's crew staying with us.

Having Pamco and other corporate guests during the winter season encouraged me to write a business plan that would touch not only on the spiritual aspects of the Double K Ranch but also our business ideas for the future. I wanted to outline the plans for the development of the business while describing the ambience of the establishment. I thought if we set these goals, and were successful on our own for five years, someone might be willing to lend us money for major maintenance or expansion.

The plan would also carefully define the direction I wanted for the ranch. My idea of a retreat for ministers and churches was all but dead. No ministers had ever come and only one church group had made use of the facility. Instead we were serving the needs of other institutions and non-profit organizations. They recognized that the ranch offered an intimate surrounding with multiple opportunities for recreation, natural beauty, and a place to meet without interruptions.

I sat for days trying to use information, gathered over several weeks, to write a clear and concise business-like report. My writing came off as stiff and indifferent or too sweet and cute. I needed to find a happy medium in my writing or someone to help me.

Two friends of ours, Eileen and Steve, owned a marketing and publicity firm, and I asked them to help. They weren't able to do it, but had an employee, Linda, who agreed to take on the project. She was impressed with all the materials I had collected. She asked questions about my vision for the ranch in two, three and five years and then we worked backward figuring out what I needed to do and in what time frame to achieve that vision.

A business plan was born. It took the form of a booklet printed in forest green ink with big letters spelling out "DOUBLE K BUSINESS PLAN". Each page was filled with my hopes and dreams for the ranch couched in words that made it sound official but with a softer feel. Linda had created a masterpiece from the material.

I sat and read it many times over the next few days. It was a tremendous step toward feeling professional and putting meat on the bones of my ideas. Written down, the ideas seemed more attainable than they had rumbling around in my head.

Linda didn't stop with the writing. She suggested to the local TV station that they do a short piece on the Double K and they came and filmed the segment. It was very short but free and a means of advertising what we were doing in the mountains.

Feeling more confident in my abilities as an innkeeper and following the chapter in my business plan entitled *Publicity;* I placed ads in the Seattle Sunday paper. They were small, designed by me, and checked over by Linda. The ads looked so good I had them inserted in the *Washington Business Monthly* and *Washington Magazine*. Because of those ads, the Double K was included in an article in the *Washington Business Monthly* about business retreat sites in the state. Compared to other places, the ranch was very small and rustic, but it didn't matter, we were in the article and that was exciting.

The ads brought new contacts and guests for both spring and summer. I received many inquiries about the following winter season, too. This upsurge in activity cushioned the departure of the Pamco group. I had mixed feelings about their leaving. I felt a great debt of gratitude toward the company for helping us to survive financially and to the crew for being so patient, willing to entertain Katy, and being a part of our family, not just "guests."

At the same time I was relieved. I wouldn't have to fix breakfast every morning at six, pack lunches, cook a special evening meal every night, or rush around on Monday trying to get the place ready for their return. If I wanted to serve my family pancakes for dinner some nights, I would be free to do that. It was the feeling I imagined moms have when their children are finally "out of the nest."

I wouldn't see the men again, not in the same kind of relationship we had while they stayed. I believed the threads of life we wove together over that winter season would always be part of who we were as the Double K.

Chapter Twenty-Seven
COMMUNITY CENTRAL

The Goose Prairie Inn sat at the side of Bumping River Road about two thirds of the way to the lake and a short walk from the Double K. Two railings running the length of the porch served as a hitching post for dogs when their owners went in for morning coffee. The old screen door banged shut every time someone went in or out.

Bar stools, wobbly from frequent use, lined the counter just inside the door. Shelves to the right were stocked with items like canned fruits and vegetables, packaged pastry tarts, diapers, bright blue tarps, fishing tackle, matches and small beach toys. To the left of the counter was a small room with tables and chairs, long window seats, and a pot-bellied stove, a godsend in October and November when the wind whipped through the prairie bringing rain and snow. A great co-mingling of smells, bacon, coffee and toast, cigarettes, and sweat permeated the air and gave the restaurant an ambience all its own.

From the window seats we could see who was coming and going. Most local people stopped by the store on their way in or out of Goose Prairie to hear the latest news. Visitors came by hoping to find an indoor toilet or a payphone.

Going to the Goose Prairie Inn was a daily treat. Between nine and ten a.m. local people would begin to wander in. The men usually assembled at the counter while the women sat around the first table. Sharing community and personal news was our priority. Potlucks were planned, serious family matters discussed and yes, there was a little gossip. We laughed about the odd requests made by strangers for tours of our homes, the vehicles stuck in the mud or snow on the primitive mountain roads above us, or the audacity of visitors wanting to use the non-existent home telephones. We helped ourselves to the coffee as we needed it and whoever paid first usually paid for the others' coffee.

Sometimes we splurged and had toast with the coffee. If we were really hungry or there was lots of information to share we'd have breakfast or stay for lunch. We didn't do that too often because Denny or Darlene, the owners, would have to be out in the kitchen rather than visiting with us.

Some folks who stopped by for coffee had annoying habits. One man in particular sat at the counter and expected to be waited on immediately. When he finished his coffee, he tilted his cup back and forth tapping it on the counter at each tilt to get Darlene's attention. If that didn't do the trick, he tapped on the cup with his spoon until she filled it.

The restaurant was always full and the store very busy on summer weekends. Denny had to cook constantly while Darlene waited on tables and served as cashier. The busyness of the weekends made coffee hour on Monday all the more sweet. Campgrounds had emptied the night before, weekend prairie people went home, and the daily traffic was at a minimum. We lingered longer, caught up on all the news and Denny and Darlene could join us without having to jump up to wait on customers.

During hunting season, we moved our seats of operation. In late October and November, it was too cold and windy to sit by the door or even at the first table. We moved back by the woodstove, huddling closer to stay minimally warm, hoping the fire would get bigger before our toes froze. The conversation varied a little because there were so few people left by then and most of the visitors were hunters up for the seasonal kill.

"Bow season" came first. These hunters appeared in camouflage clothing, their faces and hands covered in black dust. Carrying their bows and arrows over their shoulders, they looked like people gone astray from an ancient war game. Gun hunters came next and they were a scary lot. Some of them drank late into the night and went hunting with powerful rifles at dawn, still intoxicated from the night before. Drinking began again as the sun appeared over the horizon.

The hunters ordered large breakfasts and sat for hours trying to get warm after a long morning of following elk or deer. They would often drink beer along with the eggs and bacon and after a glass or two the animals they had hunted got bigger and their adventure stories more dangerous. It was great entertainment on cold, rainy mornings in November.

As dark approached in the afternoon the store would empty, but some of the hunters came back in late evening ready for another hot meal. Others went down to Whistlin' Jack to watch television at night. To avoid losing business, Denny decided to get a big screen TV, which ran off the generator. He purchased a satellite dish that got more stations than Whistlin' Jack and business in the evening picked up.

Katy always wanted to stop in after school during hunting season. She loved Darlene and Denny and liked being part of the action at the Inn. She watched the hunters and told Darlene about her day at school. Sometimes she got to wipe down tables, pour coffee, or wear an apron just like Darlene and that made her late afternoon very special.

Although there weren't other children with whom to trick-or-treat, Katy enjoyed Halloween because the neighbors doted on her. She went to three or four houses and at each one she was given bags of chocolate, hard candies, and all kinds of full-size candy bars. She would hurry over to the store and dump it all out so everyone could see her haul.

One year, after Halloween, Katy spent a lot of time at the Inn wearing the tiara from her princess costume. The hunters were most gracious and complimented her on it every day. They made up stories about princesses and told her that her prince was coming on a white horse. Her head was still holding up that tiara the following spring when the store re-opened for the season. Towards the beginning of summer it came off and we never saw it again.

The Goose Prairie Inn closed at the end of hunting season. Denny and Darlene took much needed time off. Some residents closed up their places for the winter and headed back to Yakima or to the other side of the mountains. Others traveled south to warmer climates. For those who stayed the work of maintaining our properties during the storms and cold kept us from getting together at each other's houses as often as we would have liked. So the opening of the store heralded spring's arrival and renewed friendships.

The Inn opened again in May for Mother's Day. Darlene got the stored merchandise out of mouse-proof containers and brought in all the things she had ordered over the winter. Old friends returned after a long winter's break and we got in the coffee habit again. There was family news, winter vacation highlights to discuss, and prairie gossip. Who was selling? Who was sick? Who might not come up in the summer?

What was so wonderful about the store and the coffee hour was it helped mark the seasons by more than weather. Without consciously doing it, Denny and Darlene were the log keepers of where people were, when they would get back, and how long they would be gone. They were the message center for delinquent hikers, sheriff's deputies, and lost dogs. Without them and the store, daily life wouldn't have been half the fun.

Chapter Twenty-Eight

FOOD, GLORIOUS FOOD

E ight-hundred dollars!"
Bold-numbered signs shot up around the room as the auctioneer hollered out the rising bid on the item before the audience. Great food and lots of liquor had preceded this auction. Business people, who at other times would have been very cautious, were throwing it to the wind and forcing the bidding up beyond our expectations.

Tom and I had agreed to offer a weekend stay at the ranch, including a gourmet dinner served beside a roaring fire, as an auction item in the Yakima Rotary Club's gala money raising event. Tom had been reluctant, but I thought it would be fairly successful, especially with those who knew and loved Goose Prairie. And now the bidding was almost at a thousand dollars.

A businessman from Yakima made the final bid. Tom and I knew him as fun loving. He would bring people who were similar in character and style. I was thrilled with the amount of money our weekend at the Double K brought in for the Rotary Club and pleased that our first foray into gourmet dinners and special guest weekends would be with people we knew rather than with strangers.

A side benefit to this Rotary offering was a change in attitude by our friends and acquaintances. Perhaps it was only a change in my mind, but I felt an acceptance in the community I hadn't experienced before. It was a subtle shift, but it made me feel like they now believed in us and considered we were making a valuable commitment to the Yakima Valley. Before the auction we were kept at an emotionally safe distance. Everyone who knew us knew Tom's employer moved people every five to seven years. With the purchase of the ranch and this gift to the community fund-raising event, we had made a statement of our intent. We were settling here, at least for a while and were doing it in a way that connected us to the Valley's history.

Perhaps the change was in me. I had not put down roots strongly in the past, and this was a commitment on my part to the larger community around me. Whatever it was, I liked it. I felt like a contributor to the present and future of this part of Washington State and there was a certain pride in that undertaking.

Several days before the Rotary weekend, Tom and I prepared the menu for an epicurean dinner. Tom had spent the winter months of previous years cutting out recipes from newspaper food sections and Gourmet Magazine and filed them in white binders. He had sorted the recipes into categories like chicken, beef, soup, vegetables or dessert and then within each category had filed them by the specific cut of meat, type of vegetable, or kind of dessert. Although I had poked fun at him while he assembled "the binders" (as he called them), I truly appreciated being able to find a recipe for almost any kind of food in a short time. All our chosen recipes for the gourmet dinner came from his beloved binders.

The Rotary group arrived late one Saturday morning in January, deposited their bags in the guest rooms, and went out to spend the rest of the snowy day skiing.

Tom and I chopped vegetables, made the desserts and did all the last minute food preparations for dinner. We moved one of the dining tables into the living room, placed it close to the fireplace, and set it with our best linens and antique china. Tom built a spectacular fire with huge log pieces. The soft, diffused light of the gas lamps wrapped the living room in the ambience of candlelight.

By the time dinner was served, our guests were excited and so were we. Beginning with a beautiful red and green pepper bisque soup, one color on each side of the bowl, and ending with a flambéed pear and ice cream dessert, the dinner was exquisite. Our guests went to bed that night feeling nourished, both in body and mind. Totally exhausted, we crawled into bed still having enough energy to flatter ourselves on a job well done!

The Rotary weekend gave us confidence to do more gourmet-type dinners in the spring and going into summer we were feeling proud of ourselves. Then in July a group from Tennessee arrived. It consisted of the mother and aunts of a young woman from Seattle who had convinced her female relatives to tour the Northwest. She had asked a friend to make the arrangements, hire a van, and take care of things in general so she could enjoy being with her relatives. The aunts plopped themselves into chairs in the great room as soon as they arrived and began pulling what looked like newspapers from their overstuffed purses. The "Daily Star," "Inquirer," and "The Globe" were handed one to another until each woman was pleased with her choice, took her shoes off, and lost contact with the world as she delved into the star-studded gossip pages.

Every once in a while I could hear the daughter and her friend ask them if they wanted to take a trip, go for a hike, or walk around the property. Each time the answer was a polite no, until the aunts agreed that a short trip to the lake would be suitable. I watched from the window as they piled back into the van, purses and newspapers in tow, and drove down the driveway.

Elegant northwest cuisine was on the menu for their dinner and highlighted fresh fish and locally grown vegetables. I carefully cut out triangles from parchment paper, covered each piece with hand-julienned steamed vegetables and a light sauce. On top, I placed a piece of beautiful pink salmon and folded the edges of the parchment over the fish. The bundles looked like mini gift packages.

As the guests sat down for dinner, I proudly served the salmon "en papillote" along with steamed new potatoes and fresh green beans. There was a collective "ah" as they began slicing the little packets open with their knives. The three southern aunts looked inside and there was a hushed pause. Obviously my fine work in the kitchen was a brilliant success. I beamed as the oldest aunt lifted her head and stared at me.

"E-uuuu, we don't eaht fisssh…."

Leftover meatloaf from guests the night before got heated and the ladies enjoyed leftovers while the rest of us feasted on extra salmon filets. I reassessed my menu for the following nights and stuck with meat and potatoes.

Children presented an entirely different problem. They didn't like some of the food I served at the ranch, but they were willing to eat peanut butter or grilled cheese at *every* meal. Most of the parents viewed time at the ranch as a vacation and relaxed the rules on what their children had to eat so peanut butter or grilled cheese was fine. Others, sticking to a customary routine, brought approved snacks for the children and quietly added them to the food on the table. But sometimes the parents were the problem and we got to observe family dynamics over a meal.

There was one little girl who ate nothing but peanut butter and was quite happy with her choice. But instead of leaving her alone to eat it, her parents made a fuss over her while we were eating.

"Mary Margaret," her mother would coo, "you should eat something else, honey bee."

"I just want peanut butter." Mary Margaret piled it high on the white bread.

Her father added his chorus. "Oh my, I just don't know how you'll grow into a beautiful young lady on peanut butter. Why don't you have some salad?"

"I don't like salad. I don't like meat. I'm not eating those vegetables." Mary Margaret wielded her knife, squishing the fresh white bread, peanut butter oozing off the sides. She put the knife down, licked her fingers, broke the bread apart, and stuffed the first quarter into her mouth.

"My, my, Mary Margaret. Eight years old and all you eat is peanut butter. What are we going to do with you?"

I could barely contain my own comments, which would have been directed at the parents. Katy, who at nine was just a year older than Mary Margaret, looked at me, one corner of her mouth quivering. She was exerting great energy to hold in her laughter.

Another set of guests brought different complications.

"Oh, by the way, I'm a vegetarian."

Five minutes before the meal Joseph, a man who had been at the ranch with a group several times before, announced his dietary change.

"When did you become a vegetarian, Joseph?"

"Oh, I've been one since college."

College? Every other time he had visited the ranch he had eaten bacon or sausage for breakfast, and roast beef, pork chops or stew for dinner. Although the ranch's literature stated very clearly that we could accommodate special diets with a week's notice and were more than happy to do so, many people came and expected an adjustment to the menu immediately. For these people I began keeping tofu.

It came in sealed "last-forever" packages and some brands didn't even need refrigeration. My theory was that a real vegetarian would eat tofu without a problem and the fly-by-night version would gag at the thought. It wasn't the best hospitality and I only used the ploy once. Joseph never claimed to be a vegetarian again.

My favorite guests were the birds who came to roost on the feeder outside the dining room windows. They ate a variety of foods but stuck mostly with whole grains and were true vegetarians. Each morning I set their little tabletop with cereal, seeds, pieces of fruit, and anything else I thought would appeal to them. They flew in from all directions, sat at the edge of the table, and ate to their heart's content. Sometimes a rowdy, feathered neighbor would push and shove, doing a little grapevine-step to knock away the other bird roosting next to him on the table's edge.

In summer, squirrels ran up the feeder's single post, willing to chance a surprise attack from the Canadian Jays who were staking their territory on the platform above. In winter snow, the squirrels waited patiently below for the birds' prancing dance on the table. The footloose frenzy scattered snow and food which fell to the ground where the waiting squirrels darted around filling their mouths with each morsel accidentally kicked to them. The pecking order was in full swing when the dogs got out and greedily licked up all the food the squirrels couldn't stuff in their mouths before fleeing their larger opponents.

After weeks of putting food out and inching closer to the feeder, I could finally stand right next to it as the birds ate. Eventually the brave little birds landed on my arms and took food out of my hands. I loved looking at them up close, to discern small characteristics that made each bird unique and identify them day after day as they returned to the feeder.

How different humans and animals were at the ranch. People were fussy about the food but willing to let others partake. Animals and birds ate anything, but weren't willing to share. Blending the characteristics of these species might bring about a more perfect world.

Chapter Twenty-Nine

RENOVATIONS

The dark and dingy lodge kitchen needed an overhaul. It had the potential to be a good working space, but the previous owners had not realized it. The kitchen was small, about the size of two walk-in closets put end to end, but it opened to the dining room, which made it seem more spacious.

The countertops were covered in three different patterns of floor linoleum and the floor linoleum itself was different than the other three. Every shade of dull green imaginable was included in these different patterns. The linoleum on the counter surfaces was worn in several places. The unfinished edges curled inward and the exposed seams were chipped. Metal strips, holding the linoleum down to the countertop, were bent back at the corners. Every time someone passed by the counter edge there was a loud and prolonged ripping sound as the metal tentacle grabbed shirttails or jeans' pocket and ripped them from the main part of the garment.

In some places the linoleum on the floor was worn through to wood. It curled up along some of the floor edges posing a tripping danger whenever we walked in or out of the kitchen. In some places the pattern was not even evident.

The galvanized, three-unit sink under the kitchen window was rusty and showing its age. The sinks were square and deep with a metal drain board at each end. The whole unit stood on thin legs balanced on a piece of plywood raised off the floor by pieces of four by four. This little platform was closed in along the bottom offering two inches of airspace between the flooring and the plywood supporting the sink. The whole unit, including the inside of the sinks, was covered with a dull gray marine paint. It was peeling and in the little peeled-paint cracks and crevices rust had formed. The metal splashboard behind the sinks had not been painted and was in good condition compared to the rest of the unit.

Long drawers ran under the counter next to the sink. The top drawers were sectioned off for silverware and utensils. The lower drawers were deep bins which sealed well when closed, making them rodent proof. The cabinets over the counter rose almost to the ceiling and were made of thick planks of wood running about eight feet along the wall. There were no doors on the cabinets, which was convenient for getting dishes out and putting them away, but not very hygienic because of the dust that settled on them, especially in summer.

Dividing the kitchen and the dining room was a large low cabinet with a big counter top and open storage below. It was very wide and nothing in the back on the shelves could be reached easily. It was moveable, but the dirt pile-up in the corners and around the legs due to wax build-up over many years was disgusting. The countertop was six inches lower than the regular countertops and working on it was not comfortable. It, too, was covered with different patterned linoleum.

The refrigerator at the far end of the kitchen operated on propane. It stood on top of a heavy-duty wooden crate, putting it at a more convenient level. The space inside the refrigerator was limited and even more so when ice formed on the back of the top shelf. The freezer worked well at all times, but in the tiny space there was only room for a few ice cube trays and perhaps a half-gallon ice cream container.

The first two years we made do with the kitchen as it was, but after a good winter business we decided to re-do the flooring and get rid of the big moving cabinet. Real counters, shelves and storage would replace it. I needed a higher counter that created a more hygienic environment when guests were around keeping them away from the food while it was being prepared. A half-size, propane refrigerator and a small gas stove would be included in the remodel as well, for extra storage and an option to firing up the wood stove.

New flooring signaled the beginning of the project. Tom and I had to move the low cabinet and the woodstove ourselves because the flooring men didn't do that kind of work. First, we moved the cabinet out into the dining room, which was a little tricky around the four by four center post dividing the kitchen from the dining room. The big challenge was moving the woodstove out into the dining room and back without damaging the new floor.

Tom rented two dollies and four jacks. We put a jack under each corner of the stove hoping the weight of the stove wouldn't cause the jack to go through the metal bottom of the ovens. We slipped the dollies under each side of the stove and slowly lowered the jacks until the full weight of the stove rested on the dollies. The legs were off the floor. So far, so good.

As we began to push, pull and shove the stove we found that once it got rolling it moved easily and quickly with the momentum of its weight. A little too quickly, we headed across the kitchen floor and passed the opening. We pushed it back a little more slowly.

The beam post in the middle of the floor again presented a problem. Soon we realized we had to turn the stove ninety degrees to get the it around the beam. The dollies didn't turn so we had to jack the woodstove back up, take the dollies out, turn them and then turn the stove out into the dining room. Getting it back in over the new floor was going to demand even more ingenuity.

The men came to rip up the old flooring and in doing so found that a new sub floor was needed. It was put in and the linoleum laid. It looked superb and brightened the kitchen considerably. But it also added an inch lip to the kitchen areas. It felt like a steep incline as we worked to get the half-ton stove back into place. But somehow we managed.

Next we tried to get several bids for the counters and work area reconstruction. We seemed to be good at securing people to come and look at the work possibility, but no one wanted to do the job. It wasn't a large job and it was low budget. We also would not allow smoking on the work site. Finally, a local builder, with a fine reputation and whose work we admired, come to give us a bid. He was willing to do the work but let us know that he was booked for quite a while. We assured him we understood. He was the most promising candidate yet. Several weeks passed and we were beginning to think that he too had abandoned us and the project. At last he called to say he could fit us in at the end of May and the beginning of June. It would take him ten days. Ten days, I thought. I can live with a torn apart kitchen for ten days.

The builder would start the weekend before Memorial Day and would be working at our house the next weekend as well. We had a large group coming in on the third of June. I counted the days and noted that the kitchen would most likely be done at least a week before that. Great.

The Saturday of Memorial Day weekend arrived and so did the building materials and the builder. He was careful as he worked, cleaning up as he went and apologizing for the dust and dirt wafting through the house. When evening came he dusted the counters, swept the floor and put all his tools to one side of the kitchen area.

On Sunday he showed up and followed the same routine as the day before, ripping out counters, getting the measurements for cabinets he was building. I believed he was getting ready for the nine days ahead. Sunday night he packed up his things, put everything away and said, "See you next weekend." Next weekend? What about the week? He explained that he had a big job over on the other side of the mountains and that we, being a small job, would be fit in on the weekends.

In retrospect, I was lucky. Had I insisted on ten days in a row, my project would not have been started until the next spring. In the midst of the mess, knowing that in less than two weeks I had to cook a dinner for forty people and accommodate twenty people for ten days, I was less than thrilled. But not a word came out except "thank you. See you next weekend."

Each weekend went according to the builder's plan. Cabinets were made and installed and the plywood counter tops put in place. All the fittings for the refrigerator and stove were installed as well, and our remodeled kitchen began taking shape.

On the weekend of the dinner for forty, a friend came to help cook. We fired up the woodstove to cook two large pork roasts. Rice pilaf and assorted side dishes needing little space for preparation and storage were prepared. During the course of the preparation (done on top of the bare plywood, recently installed) I spilled all of the grease out of the meat pan. For a few weekends we not only had the sounds of the saw and the mess of the dust, but also the smell of rendered pork fat. The dinner guests worked around the mess and seemed quite amused by it all. No one seemed to mind the chaos except me.

To save money on this project, Tom did the plumbing for the new sink unit. He started the day after the dinner party. He got a few of his friends and colleagues who were staying with us to remove the old galvanized sinks and switch the plumbing to more modern pipe and fillings. When they pulled the sink and the shelving that had been built a few inches from the floor, they discovered a mouse nest. Rather, it was more like an apartment complex in miniature. Those cheese curls from our first adventurous day were under there as well as assorted string, dust, rug strands and food. Comfy little place for small critters. We swept it all out and made sure any holes from the basement were plugged.

Installing the new sink took lots of supervision by Tom. The friends would get the pipes fitted and then find it leaked because the fittings had been put on upside down. Then the fitting at the hot water control went bad and since they were washer-less faucets Tom had to run to town and get a whole new fixture.

The counter tops were covered with the laminate, the refrigerator installed, and the gas oven set into the new wooden structure built where the moveable cabinet had been. I made new red and white curtains for the windows and the space under the sink to make the room look more inviting.

The kitchen was complete. New countertops, a gas stove, non-rusty sinks and a small refrigerator to hold the overflow of food along with pullout shelves and lots of new cabinets, made the weeks of waiting truly satisfying. Cooking became more fun and less laborious and I truly felt like a gourmet chef.

Chapter Thirty

ALIENATION OF ONE

G athering a small crew of young adult Scouts (who loved any excuse to come to the mountains to work and share a good meal), we began construction of a large deck off the dining room. Forty concrete supports, one every measured foot, had to be placed as designated in the plan. The young men, shirts off even in the cool mountain air, huffed and puffed moving blocks until they were in the exact spot, lined up with the string and pegs Tom had placed earlier.

We hadn't had rain for several weeks, but raindrops fell intermittently throughout the day. By the time dinner was ready, and everyone sat down to eat, it was raining hard. Sunday's work had to be postponed.

The next weekend some of the same guys came back to help. It hadn't rained all week, but on that Saturday, clouds and wind, as well as misty rains slowed the progress of laying the support beams on the concrete blocks. The volunteers prevailed and most of the work got done, but I could tell their enthusiasm for the project was waning and they were growing weary of riding home in their cars or on motorcycles in wet clothes. Tom and I finished the support beams ourselves and began to cut two-by-fours for the next weekend. We planned to lay the decking, build the benches for seating, and put up the railing.

I got up early the following Saturday. Although the sky was overcast and threatening, no rain was expected. One helper showed up but could only stay until noon. We began placing the two-by-fours, making sure the space between each of the boards was uniform. Place, space, and hammer. Place, space, and hammer. Six hours later, almost half of the decking wood was installed. Pain was shooting up my back from bending over, but there was also a feeling of satisfaction from seeing the deck take shape. Tom and I stopped work and agreed to begin early the next morning.

Sunday was as overcast as Saturday. No one came to help. My body was sore, but since we were so close to finishing with the boards, I felt motivated to get the work done. As soon as we began, the rain started again. Tom asked if I would like to stop and go in, but I wanted to finish. I felt very single-minded about it and began to think of my arms and hands as a nailing machine.

The dogs stayed with Tom and me as we worked. Conversation remained at a minimum as the rhythm of laying the boards, spacing and nailing took over. Wet clothes stuck to my legs and back, water from my hair dripped into my eyes and ears, and drops of moisture on the hammer and nails made them slippery and hard to manage. I worked faster as the rain came down harder and harder.

Turning to get more nails, I saw someone coming up the lane on a bicycle. A small dog was running alongside. Bear, who was not fond of other dogs on her property, stood at attention, ears back, ready to ward off the strange animal. I stood up, quickly grabbing her collar as she began to bark.

"Can't you read?" I yelled. I couldn't see the face of the person from the deck without my glasses. "The sign says 'no trespassing'. Get that dog away from here." Bear had already attacked the small dog of another property owner who brought her dog onto our land though we had warned her not to.

I looked at Tom to see what he was going to do about the situation. He stood there looking at me, and then looked at the man on the bike. Obviously, Tom was not going to do anything so I continued.

"Hey, you, you're trespassing!" I turned to Tom and mumbled, "What kind of nitwit is bringing that dog up here without permission?"

Tom stared at me and then replied. "It's our neighbor, Kathleen." He seemed stunned by my yelling. "He's in Rotary with me."

By now, the cyclist had slowed, stopped and picked up the dog. I pulled Bear toward the house and put her inside. Rain and deck construction had finally gotten to me. I was the nitwit. Approaching the man and dog, I assumed my most humble posture.

"I am *so* sorry for yelling. I didn't know who you were until Tom explained. We have so many strangers coming up to look in the windows and wander around." Such a feeble apology, but I felt like the woman from the black lagoon, soaking wet and tired.

"Kathleen, this is Ken. His family has the cabin on the next lane." There was a long pause. "This is my wife, Kathleen." I'm sure this was a proud moment for my husband, having to introduce the screaming woman as his wife. We made some polite small talk, but the atmosphere was strained. A short time later, we said goodbye, and headed back to work.

That evening the deck was done. The rain had stopped and we sat on the nailed boards, admiring our work. I had never worked on a project like this and the satisfaction was tremendous. Every three minutes I told Tom how beautiful the deck was and how proud I felt. We had done it ourselves.

"Yeah," he said, "and to think you only alienated one neighbor in the process!"

Ah, the neighbor. Tomorrow would be soon enough to assess the damage I had done. Along with building the benches and steps for the deck, I had some fences to mend. A hot shower and a good night's sleep would fortify me for the work ahead.

Chapter Thirty-One

FRIENDLY GET-TOGETHERS

Reunions at the Double K were exuberant and exciting. Family members or groups of friends came to have a good time, brought their own entertainment, and were relaxed in the matter of schedules for meals and activities. I packed lunches for them and off they went for hikes or boat rides, sometimes even a horseback ride into the mountains. In the evenings, lively games of dominoes, cards, charades, or the newest team-type guessing games were played.

Even though everyone understood that the lights would go out at ten p.m. there was always the surprised "oh's" from the second floor as guests, who were in the middle of brushing their teeth or figuring out where they had packed their night clothes, got caught in the dark. Sometimes there was silence, then a scared cry followed by peals of laughter as relatives sneaked up on each other in the dark hallway. And, after their first night of sharing the many peculiarities of the ranch like shared bathrooms, common meals, and lights out at ten, there seemed to be a closer camaraderie than when they arrived.

Katy jumped right into the midst of these family gatherings. She loved the size of these families and the fact that there was always someone paying attention to her. From the earliest age, Katy was skilled at conversation and knew just what to say to make her way into the group. They invited her to participate in all their planned activities.

She left in the morning to join in the day's happenings, sat with the group at meals, and fell into bed late at night exhausted from keeping up with all the activities. At the end of the weekend, Katy found her way into the group photos, which made me laugh. I knew in twenty years they would look at the picture and wonder who the little girl was standing in the midst of the relatives.

One remarkable group of people from Seattle adopted her immediately. They were owners or CEO's of large companies or had established themselves as knowledgeable people in their fields. She, at age eight, went skiing with them, chatted at mealtimes as if they had been her friends for years, and entertained them with her violin playing and singing while one woman in the group became her accompanist for an evening concert. The friendship blossomed over the next year and Katy ended up staying in Seattle with one family for two days. The group's women members had a little party at a famous coffee place in her honor and she got to be queen for a day.

But all groups were not the same. Sometimes Katy would join a group when they first arrived. Shortly after, she headed straight to the apartment. She ate with them because that was our rule but, when a meal was over, she went back down to the apartment or outside to visit a neighbor. Her intuition told her the group was not going to be fun (or her idea of fun) and she wanted nothing to do with them again. She never said a word about them, but more often than not, her reaction was confirmed at the end of their visit by our own conclusions. The group wasn't flexible, they expected to be entertained, took advantage of our service by having us watch their children for an hour and showing up two hours late, or complained about things over which we had no control (like the weather). They *weren't* fun and we were relieved when they left.

During the summer of 1994, we hosted a tour from a business called "Outdoor Vacations for Women Over Forty." Thirteen women, over the age of forty, came from all over the country for a week of easy mountain adventure. The planning took months, but it was fun to arrange hiking, trekking at Mt Rainier, visits to old west towns, and a luncheon in a spectacular winery garden in the Yakima Valley. I asked the mother of one of Katy's friends to come each day to clean and begin meal preparation while I hauled the women around in a rented van. All went well until next to the last day.

Right after breakfast, I asked everyone to be out at the van in fifteen minutes. When we were all assembled, one of the women counted "heads" and all were present. I ran into the house to get the snacks as the group piled into the vehicle. Closing the doors, I asked again if everyone was present and, on hearing yes, headed down the driveway.

I drove for about a half hour up steep mountain roads that turned to dirt about halfway up. We met the guide and got the directions for the morning hike. Just as we were ready to begin, one of the women rushed up to me.

"Have you seen Dee?"

"No," I said. "Did she go ahead of the group?" I looked around quickly and felt the color rise in my face.

"Attention, ladies." Has anyone seen Dee?" They looked around and began to shake their heads.

"She got out of the van to get a hat. I thought she got back in. Maybe not."

They looked at one another then at me, as the realization hit. We had left her at the ranch!

Leaving the group with the guide, I drove as fast as I could down the mountain. I felt sweaty and nervous. How, after counting twice and asking everyone if the whole group was present, had I left someone? The whole way back, I analyzed the situation, shoring myself up mentally then tearing my own defense down.

Approaching the house, I girded myself for what I felt would be an angry confrontation. Calm, I thought to myself. Stay calm, and get her to the group as fast as possible. As I got out of the van, the front door opened and Dee came out.

"Hey, where have you been? I waited down by the mailbox for a while, and then realized you all weren't coming back. I'll tell you, I'm mad, especially at my best friend. She didn't even notice I was gone!"

"I am so sorry. I counted twice and asked if everyone was present and they all said yes. I should have counted again." We climbed into the van and headed down the driveway.

"Don't worry. I'm not mad at you. It's those friends of mine. I told them I had to go back and get a hat and they forgot. Forgot right away. Some friends!"

Relief. In her eyes, I wasn't to blame, so the trip back up the mountain was good. We decided not to catch up, but rather hike the route backwards and join the others wherever we met. She did give her friends a hard time when we finally joined them, but the surrounding mountain beauty and the gentle breeze filled with the scent of pine dissipated the frustration and hurt. By the time the hike was over, all was forgiven!

A group from southern Washington came in August for a weekend. On Saturday morning I packed their lunches and asked them what the plan was for the day.

"We're headed up to Copper City," said Kent. "Can you tell us the best way to go?"

"Are you hiking up?" It would take the group most of the day once they left the main road.

"No, we're driving the pick-up as far as we can and then hiking from there."

"How many are going? Everyone?" They had a group of twelve and I knew they couldn't all ride in one truck.

"We're going to sit in the back."

"That's dangerous on these bumpy mountain roads." And everywhere else, I thought. I wasn't in charge of the group's activity but this made me feel uneasy. My facial expression must have given away my feelings.

"We'll all be sitting down and Rob said he'd drive very slowly. We'll be very careful, I promise."

They gathered up the lunches, bottles of water, and their daypacks, and headed out the door. From the front porch I watched them climb into the truck and sit in rows on the flat bed. I hoped they would be safe. The truck drove slowly down the drive as the passengers laughed and sang and waved good-bye to me.

I spent the next two hours cleaning the kitchen and the great room. It was a spectacular day and I wanted to get finished so I could spend some time outdoors myself. I was mopping the bathroom floors when I heard the back screen door bang. No one was supposed to be in the lodge. Tom and Katy were at the camp and the group was hiking.

"Hey, Kathleen! Are you here?" It was Sara, a member of the hiking group.

"Upstairs in the bathroom." I went to the top of the stairs and she came bounding up two at a time. She looked very worried. "What's up?"

"Kent fell off of the truck. He was unconscious for a few minutes and now he says his neck hurts and he can't move."

I put the mop in the bucket and headed down the stairs with her.

"We'll call the medics on the radio phone. How far did you get before this happened?"

"The truck is at the trailhead. We got there safely and all sat still until Rob turned off the ignition. Kent was the first one to stand up and when he did, Rob took his foot off the brake and the truck rolled backward slightly, throwing Kent to the ground. We weren't even moving when it happened!" She was starting to cry. I put my arm around her and gave her a brief hug.

"I'll call the fire department and give them the information we have. We'll meet the paramedics at the trailhead. I presume you brought the truck back down?" She nodded.

The connection on the radio phone was good and I reached the fire department immediately. We left the ranch and headed to the Copper City trailhead where the rest of the group was waiting. Kent was awake, but ashen in color and chilled. His friends had covered him with their light jackets and were huddled around him providing comforting words.

In a short time, we heard the faint sound of a siren from the valley below. It got louder as it ascended the mountain road. When the ambulance arrived, two paramedics got out, asked everyone to step back and talked softly to Kent as they assessed his condition. They got a board and a collar from the ambulance and stabilized his neck and spine as he lay on the ground.

"Who phoned us?"

"I did. This group is staying at the Double K and I'm the owner."

"We'd like to talk to you, please."

I walked over to the back of the ambulance where the two medics were now standing.

"We don't think it would be good to put him in the unit and drive down the road. It's too bumpy and we're not sure whether his neck or his back is broken. We are going to have to bring in the medical helicopter from the base. But we need to call and can't get any reception up here on our phones."

"I brought the radio phone. Use it." He took it from me and I gave him instructions.

I wondered how they would land a helicopter in the trees. When he got off the phone, he told us they thought they could land in the clearing as he had described it. They would do a "fly-over" and make sure. All we could do now was wait and hope Kent's condition didn't deteriorate.

The sound of the whirling rotors brought us out of our somber mood. Who wouldn't be excited about a helicopter landing in a clearing in the mountains? The helicopter came in very close and the door opened. A man leaned out and motioned for us to clear the area. He wanted the truck moved as far back as possible and for us to shield our eyes from debris created by the rotors hitting the treetops. It was an amazing feat getting that huge machine through the trees into the small clearing. As soon as the chopper touched the ground, two men jumped out, gave us a warning to stay back, and went to Kent and the two ambulance paramedics.

The four men explained the flight procedure to him, lifted him up on the medical board, and carried him to the helicopter where he was strapped into a gurney. They closed the door and the ambulance crew ran back to where we were standing. The rotors turned slowly at first and then got faster with each rotation. At top speed their power was immense and the helicopter rose straight up, barely touching the surrounding trees. As the sound faded, we thanked the ambulance crew and headed down the mountain.

The afternoon had been emotional. The joy of the reunion had been sapped from the group. After having a hot meal at the lodge, they decided to leave immediately. A stop at the hospital was planned to check on their friend before they headed home.

A week later we got news that Kent was doing well. His neck and back were not broken but injured. He was out of the hospital and would make a full recovery. It took me a few days to get over this reunion. I was not responsible for what happened and I did try to warn them about the dangers, but I still felt a twinge of guilt because it had happened while they were my guests.

This situation provided a good lesson about "inn keeping." No matter how perfect an experience I wanted someone to have, there was only so much over which I had control. The rest was up to the guest and each one had a mind of his or her own.

Chapter Thirty-Two

WATERLESS ADVENTURE

Kay and Isabelle had told us the well was at least twenty-five feet deep and far below the water table. Neophytes at water systems and wells, we believed them without checking it out ourselves. For a few years the water came out of the faucets, the toilets flushed and the washing machine filled without any trouble. Guests who came from Yakima or Seattle complimented the water, saying it was crystal clear and without the chemical taste of city water.

One day, though, the water tasted funny and had a very peculiar smell. We walked down to the well house and began searching through the underbrush and rotting leaves for the well itself. We found it a few minutes later and pulled off a three-foot square wooden lid. The well was only sixteen feet deep and lined with rotting wood instead of a metal casing. A small rodent floated on top of the water at the bottom of the well and the stench was a stronger version of the water's odor up at the house.

On one side of the well a wooden ladder went down to what seemed to be the bottom. Tom put his foot on the second rung of the ladder and swung the other foot over to climb down into the well. The first few rungs collapsed and he clutched the wooden side to keep from falling into the murky, smelly water below. Grabbing hold of the bushes and weeds around the outside of the well, he pulled himself up.

We got the rodent out using a long-handled skimmer, added lots of chlorine bleach and sealed the well up the best we could. Back at the well house we ran the water system until the odor disappeared and the water test was good. This incident was one of the first signs something major was going to have to be done to our water supply and delivery system. We ignored the problem and assumed that the temporary "fix" was good enough to be permanent. How like Kay and Isabelle we were becoming.

That summer was very dry and as we entered October there was still no heavy rain or snow in sight. I had a busy fall guest line-up and was a bit concerned about water. We asked visitors to use this precious resource wisely and October passed without any problems in the system or supply of water.

The Anderson family arrived the Monday before Thanksgiving that year. There were five adults, four cousins and one exchange student from Finland, all expecting to have the mountain vacation of their lives. As I worked in the kitchen and spent time visiting with the relatives, I thought I heard the little generator, which ran the pump in the well house, kick on and stay on much longer than usual. But just as I became mindful of the unconscious concern, the generator shut off and I forgot about it until the next time.

That evening the temperature fell below zero Fahrenheit and within hours, the ground was frozen. Although it was cold the next day, the sky was a brilliant blue and the sun cajoled the temperature into the teens. I took the older girls to town with me and while they shopped, I taught my music students at the college. When we got home the other guests were playing dominoes and napping.

The electricity was on, providing an opportunity for me to get some wash done in the basement. I loaded the washer, turned it on and waited for it to begin to fill. It started slowly, the water trickling in to the tub.

That's odd, I thought, and watched it for a few minutes more. It got slower and finally the water stopped. The motor of the washer churned and a faint burning smell filled the air. I turned the machine off and tried the faucet at the laundry sink. A trickle, two more drops, and then nothing.

Tom, who was upstairs playing dominoes with his brothers, assumed that the pump must be broken. At the well house the pump wasn't working and there was no pressure in the pressure tank, which held the water for the house. Tom drove down to Whistlin' Jack and called the irrigation and pump company. A company representative arrived a few hours later and watched the pump for about an hour, shaking his head back and forth, shifting his weight from one foot to the other, and harrumphing occasionally.

"Your pump's not pumping water," he said. "Don't know what the problem is but I'll figure it out." I hoped he would do it soon since we were paying him by the hour beginning with his drive up to Goose Prairie from town. Two hours later, he still hadn't figured out what the problem was.

"I think you better get a new pump."

"Did you bring one with you?" Tom asked.

"Nope. Didn't know what the problem was. I could bring one up tomorrow." Tomorrow. Another four hours at sixty dollars an hour.

"Thanks, but I'll be in town and can get it myself."

"What about installation?"

"We can do it ourselves, but thanks."

It solved our problem through Thanksgiving while the relatives were visiting, but soon after there wasn't any water again. Only this time, it wasn't the pump or the pressure tank. The well had run dry. We were between groups, but in a week or so I would have a full house again and I was desperate. Lack of water meant no paying guests.

As we talked to the other Goose Prairie residents, we found they didn't have water either. With the lack of an insulating snow pack, the ground, as well as the water source several feet down, had frozen solid after several days of sub-zero temperatures. We were all in big trouble unless temperatures rose above freezing and that just wasn't likely in the near future.

As long as we didn't have guests we could manage. Tom packed empty 5-gallon containers into the truck and every night brought home water from town. We used it sparingly to cook, wash, flush, and bathe.

This kind of living demands an incredible sense of humor, an ability to see the absurd side of life, and many friends who are willing to be part of the rescue. Tom and I went to town and showered every two or three days at friends' homes. Katy still fit in the big sink in the kitchen where, with very little water, I could wash her and make it a game. She was the cleanest of all.

A group from Seattle was scheduled to come during this waterless time. It included CEOs of companies, a nationally known writer on heart disease and a woman who had a very successful import company. They had been to the ranch before in cold and snowy weather and the men, in particular, loved adventures. They also had a collective, highly tuned sense of humor. I called them and explained the situation. The men thought they would have a wonderful time. Their wives were not all that sure. But they came.

And it was an adventure. The guests couldn't shower, but we provided them with enough water to wash when necessary. There was water for coffee and tea, washing dishes and cleaning up after meals. Buckets of water to flush the toilets meant that they couldn't flush every time they used the facilities. One of the men was thrilled because it gave him an excuse to relieve himself out of the second story window at night, something he hadn't done since he was a boy. It was a funny and relaxed three days. I'm sure that any more time under these circumstances would have put everyone on edge, but the length was perfect for a waterless adventure in the mountains.

Snow finally fell the first week of December. The ground released some moisture, but, with the lack of rain or snow for so many days and the presence of rodents in the well over that time, our water supply was compromised. We had to have a new one dug by a professional. With the snow now falling and the threat of storms dumping three or four feet of snow at a time looming over us, I called several well drillers. None would risk bringing the trucks and equipment to our property, knowing there was the possibility of getting stuck there for the rest of the winter.

After many calls and lots of tears of frustration, I talked to a young man, who wavered slightly as he started to say no. I slipped into that space and promised him I would hire whatever it took to get his equipment out if it became stuck for any reason. I babbled on and on, promising him anything that would get him to say yes.

He reluctantly said okay and wanted to come right away while the ground was still fairly hard. He hoped he would hit water without having to go through much rock. I assured him he would. (What did I know?)

His trucks drove in two days later under a beautiful, sunny blue sky on a minus 10-degree day. He started to drill and I breathed a little sigh. At least he was here on our property and we would have water and business after all. I would worry about trucks and mud if and when it happened.

After a day and a half, he announced he had a good source of water about thirty five feet down, but wanted to go another ten to insure that the well would be uncompromised for a long time. The weather was warming slightly and snow clouds were beginning to move in our direction, but I was euphoric and put the dangers aside in my mind. He reached his goal on the third day and began installing the casing for the well and the submersible pump. I was thrilled. He was almost done.

As the sky began to threaten us with snow, he worked steadily. Now I began to think of the expense of getting his trucks out. Where would I find other trucks to pull him out, ones that wouldn't get stuck themselves? Most importantly, where would we get the money to pay for it all? We barely had enough to pay for the well without other unexpected expenses.

The well driller finished on the fourth day. Snow had covered the equipment the night before, but the ground was still firm and, as the trucks drove slowly off the field and down the dirt road to the pavement, I offered a silent prayer of thanks. We had water; the trucks weren't stuck in the mud and snow. We were going to be able to house the groups whose payments to the Double K would pay the well-drilling bills. This time my sigh was one of real relief.

Chapter Thirty-Three

DASHING THROUGH THE SNOW

When we first moved to Goose Prairie, I was against having a snowmobile for any purpose. That included hauling groceries or bringing guest luggage up to the lodge from the parking lot or when snow and rain made the driveway and lane nearly impassable by car or truck. I stuck with this decision until two feet of snow fell in one six-hour period and the car could no longer make it up the hill and around the circle. Groceries had to be carried an eighth of a mile uphill on slick and snowy ground. With the changing weather came a change of heart.

I watched the want ads for used snowmobiles that would be in our price range. One day a notice appeared advertising three used snowmobiles – older models from the late 70's and 80's. I called and arranged for us to see them. The next day I drove to town, picked up Tom from work and headed to a rural area close by.

We left the main road and drove up a narrow dirt lane. In front of us was an old, large, grayish-brown, shingled, two-story garage. A rock wall, a few feet away from the building, was doing its best to hold back the soil, which in turn held the building in place. We walked across a gravel path and stepped into the building. Inside my eyes adjusted to the dark.

The back wall was punctuated with old, circular black tread, steering wheels and various size hoses and drive belts. Silver, black, blue and red snowmobiles, lying upside down and on their sides, were scattered about the dirt floor, their runners pointing in all directions like the legs of tired dancers stretched and turned to ease the pain of a long performance. Hoods, windscreens and seats were missing from some of them. Several machines were parked on a crooked, wooden platform above the rest. They seemed more whole than the others.

A tall lanky man with a generous slather of grease on his shirt and dirt clumped on his overalls greeted us with a nod from a corner of the garage. He was wiping a small engine part with a grey rag. A patch of sunlight from a dirt streaked window shone on his long, bony fingers as they gently moved the cloth from side to side. He stopped and looked at us for several moments.

"Here about the snow machines, are you?"

"Yes, we called about them yesterday."

"Let me show you the ones we have." There was a pause as he took a couple strides towards the platform. "This one is slow, but it's dependable and will get you where you want to go. This one here is faster – do about forty, forty-five on a good day. Can you do your own work on em?"

"Yep," said Tom, "what kind of tools am I going to need?"

They were into "man type" conversation – tools, speed of the vehicles, engine size. I was into finding the one that suited my personality. In the corner behind several dented hoods and rusted engines was a red snowmobile. Red, especially fire engine red, was my favorite color.

"How about this red one? Is it for sale?"

I was getting kind of excited about this. I could see myself seated on this red machine, highlighted against the white snow and the deep green of the fir trees at Goose Prairie. I would be the great snowmobile adventurer – fearless, fast, and undaunted by the elements of the harshest storm.

"Yeah, I could sell you that one. Gets about twenty-five - top speed – good enough to get you around. Dependable. It's the oldest one I got that still runs. Dependable little machine. Dependable."

What is the one characteristic you have that makes you suitable for this job? His assurance of "dependable" reminded me of the answer given to that question during job interviews. The people who answer with the word "flexible" usually turn out to be the most inflexible. Would that be my experience with "dependable"? I wanted the red one anyway.Tom's interest was in a more modern snowmobile. He didn't care about the looks, but wanted something that would get him places fast. He said it needed a big engine capable of reaching sixty miles an hour on the road. One that would hold two people. This, I mentioned, meant that if we were going somewhere on the snowmobiles as a family, I would have to leave several hours before him to get there at the same time. We compromised on a heavy-duty snowmobile that could reach speeds of forty-five or fifty miles an hour with two people riding. Tom gave the owner a check and arranged a delivery date. We waited eagerly for the next decent snowfall.

During the first month we owned the snowmobiles, the county prohibited "road riding" to Bumping Lake. The snow pack was still very light so we followed a path through the forest beside the roadway. Partially broken tree branches, pushed carelessly to the ground by the heavy wet snow of the early days of winter, masked the twisted turns of the tunnel-like pathway. Patchy snow barely covered the snags and above ground tree roots. Hollow logs crisscrossed the path waiting for some ambitious rider to bring a chain saw along one day and finish the job that insects and decay had started years before. Did I have the ability to negotiate turns and anticipate these dangers? The confidence of the fast, fearless snowmobile adventurer had faded.

My first accident, a minor one, happened one snowy, overcast Saturday. I followed Tom onto the path and began to feel a little of my pre-snow confidence return. Tom, wanting to test the power of his machine was the leader. My red, slow and steady, dependable one tried to keep up. It was the story of the tortoise and the hare except the hare wasn't napping. Tom stopped occasionally and waited until I caught up, but he was having fun seeing what his machine could do. At one point he seemed to forget that I was following and as he faded out of sight, my stomach became queasy and the sides of my head began feeling like they were being squeezed very tight. I wasn't used to looking through the cloudy, plastic face of my helmet, while watching for tree branches hanging over the path. Steering this huge hunk of metal through a mess of roots, which grabbed at the machines runners like gangly fingers of a monstrous creature held captive beneath the ground's surface, I missed a hairpin turn, hit a log, flipped over the top and landed in some thick brush. The snowmobile stopped a short distance away.

I cried, not because I was hurt, but because I felt frustrated and angry at my inability to negotiate the terrain. I sat in the bushes on a small pile of wet snow, feeling sorry for myself, and a little angry with Tom for his desertion.

"Damn machine. Stupid piece of scrap metal."

I would have kicked that machine if I hadn't had to move to do it. My vision of me as a rider just didn't fit with the reality. Any more mishaps like this and my days as a snowmobiler would be brief.

The snow came on fast in the weeks following my accident. The county lifted the ban and allowed snowmobiles on the road from the beginning of Goose Prairie up to Bumping Lake and onto the Wenatchee National Forest trails beyond the lake. On the road there was safety without the worry of branches, roots and logs.

The snowmobile provided a study in tempo for my mountain symphony. As I gained speed, the wind created a deeply satisfying feeling of exhilaration, rushing over the windscreen, hitting my helmet, pushing in where my helmet was loose. I was free to zig zag down the road, make circles, double back to see the elk herd as it chanced moving in daylight high on the ridge. Revving the engine to practice a run up and across snow banks of varying heights and widths to get to the other side was joyful. At a slower pace, the newest snow line, high above on the trees along the ridges, became obvious to me. Shutting the engine down, I listened to the Canadian Jays squawk at each other from the branches above, watched the river swish its way over boulders and between river rock, and heard the high-pitched trumpeting of the elk calf echoing across the ridge when it strayed too far from the herd. From the seat of my silent snowmobile, I watched the smallest creatures, chipmunks, rabbits and mice. They crawled from nearly invisible holes in the snow, skittering here and there, scanning the forest for enemies. Sniffing the ground for food, the animals hurried onto the next burrow or hole in what I imagined was a complex underground condominium.

One afternoon I went for a solitary ride. Large snowflakes fell and stuck to the helmet face, making it difficult to see through the visor. I opened it letting the snowflakes and the cold air hit my face. I glanced at Baldy and Buffalo, the mountains rising regally on my left, fog hanging over their upper cliffs like fluffy down comforters. The tall firs and pines guarded the land between the road and the base of the mountains. Snow teetered on the ends of the tree branches and the new covering on the road made it look like unexplored territory.

At the two-mile marker, I left the road and headed into the forest on a wide logging lane. The usual rabbit and elk tracks were barely evident, the new snow providing a cover for the animals' activity. A wonderful feeling of freedom and a stirring memory of reckless youth began to rise within me as I wrapped my hand tighter around the accelerator. Part of me wanted to go faster and yet another part reminded me that a broken leg or back injury on this cold snowy day, while I was alone in the forest would be dangerous or even deadly. For a fleeting moment the embers of youthful daring flickered and almost took hold. But the dampening carefulness of middle age refused to fan the flame, fearful that the fire would rage out of control. I reached the lake and turned the snow machine toward home using the safer route along the road.

Holiday times were always good times to go riding. Although there were more snowmobiles out, there were also more people around in case of an emergency in the woods. A sense of excitement and celebration prevailed on clear, crisp and cold days during Christmas and New Year vacation times, as families and friends joined up to ride into the mountains.

On one such New Year's Day I thought it would be fun to go for a ride. The snow, light and fluffy on the top with a good solid pack underneath, was just right for riding. No one else in the family was interested in going, but I decided to go anyway, knowing from the distant sounds that there were several people out on their snowmobiles and that if I had a problem someone would stop and give me a hand. I bundled up, put on my helmet, went out and started the engine. It sounded a little sluggish, but not bad enough to cancel the ride. Bear stood in the drive, anxiously awaiting the signal that she could go along. I decided to take her.

I drove down the driveway out onto the road and headed to the lake three miles away. My top speed was the usual twenty-five miles per hour. There seemed to be snowmobiles every-where. Bear followed behind, sometimes darting into the woods, emerging several hundred feet ahead of the snowmobile a few minutes later, waiting, then following behind again.

We arrived at the lake and I stopped to admire the view across the water. Bear rested in the snow at the side of the road. The sky was a deep blue and the trees high up on the cliffs were outlined against the pure white snow on the mountains. Since the weather was so grand, I thought of leaving the paved road and going further, but Bear had been showing signs of fatigue and I wasn't sure how much further she would be able to run. I turned the snowmobile around and pulled the starter cord. Nothing happened. Again, same thing. On the third attempt the motor turned over. Bear ran ahead, excited by the engine noise. I put my helmet on and took off. The engine still didn't sound right, but I was headed home so it didn't matter.

About a mile from the lake, Bear disappeared into the woods and didn't emerge. I slowed down, circled around and waited for her to appear. No Bear. I stopped, called her, and then listened. I heard her barking in the distance down by the river. With so many snowmobiles going by I was afraid to leave her to find her way home. She might become confused and follow someone else. Reluctantly I switched the machine off and waited. After about ten minutes, Bear reappeared panting heavily, her tongue hanging out the side of her mouth. A rabbit, I thought, or even a deer. They always gave her a run for her money!

I pulled the start rope and once more the engine wouldn't turn over. Again and again I tried, but the engine wouldn't cooperate. I sat at the side of the road, watched the other snowmobiles go by in both directions and attempted to start mine again. No luck.

It was getting late and the sun was dropping low into the trees. I felt the cold in my feet and hands and as the wind picked up I knew the chill would soon spread to other parts of my body. I put the hood of my snowmobile up hoping that a passing group of snowmobilers might stop and give a hand. Two people waved, but no one stopped to help. The cold minutes ticked on.

Six riders sped by. Realizing my distress, two turned around and came back, waving their friends to go on. I told them what had happened and they pinpointed the problem, but no one was carrying the needed spark plug. As one of the men got a rope from his snowmobile, the other explained that he would tow me home. They disengaged the drive belt, and showed me how to steer without the engine running. I was concerned about Bear staying with us, but didn't think I should mention it to these helpful men who were anxious to re-join their friends. Bear would have to manage the best she could. The man towing my snowmobile revved his engine. We started off slowly until the towrope tightened. It was about thirty feet long and as we reached an easy, steady speed, my snowmobile and I seemed to be the last person on a skating whip going slowly from one side of the road to the other. It was like a beautiful Mozart andante cantabile.

This will be fine, I thought, and I started to relax. Suddenly we began going faster and faster until I felt I was on an out-of-control carnival ride. I looked back briefly and saw Bear, trying to keep up. She was getting smaller and smaller as the distance between us grew larger.

Never, in the time I had owned the snowmobile, had I gone this fast. I'm sure we were clocking at least sixty miles an hour. The man kept looking back and waving, as my snowmobile weaved back and forth across the road, no more a delicate Mozart tempo, but a Beethoven allegro con fuoco. We did not slow down until we got close to the driveway where I negotiated a wide-angle turn to prevent a crash. We arrived in the field in front of the lodge; he undid the towrope and wished me luck getting my snowmobile fixed. In a moment he was speeding back down the driveway and roaring up the road to find his friends. I had no doubt that he would catch up with them very soon.

Poor Bear. What was she thinking and what would she do? I ran up to the lodge and yelled for Tom to get his snow clothes on, take his snowmobile and find Bear. By now she was probably following someone else or feeling deserted and thoroughly lost.

Tom got ready and went out. I heard his engine crank up and the sound fade as he went down the driveway. Shortly he was back with Bear following. She had given up the chase, lay down on the snow bank and waited for me to return. I was happy she was back, glad I was home, and absolutely convinced I would never need a snowmobile that delivered a lot of speed.

Chapter Thirty-Four

SOLITUDE

I was usually unaware of the moon's fullness until the generator was shut down or the gaslights in the great room were extinguished. One particular night I found myself wishing we had a house full of people who would come outside to witness its magic, share the light's beauty and then disappear so I would be left alone with the moon like lovers conversing in silence on a darkened street.

I put on layers of clothing, heavy insulated boots, mittens, and a hat partially covering my face to protect myself from the – 20 F. cold, went out the back door of our little apartment, through the woodshed and up the driveway. The cold crystallized the snow and it sparkled as I walked along. Snow-covered tree branches were silhouetted against the ground like huge shadow-box figures. I passed the well house, crossed the small, crystal clear creek running over the driveway, and stood in the open field in front of the lodge. The moon's reflection, full and round, shone off the snow. Coming from the darkness of the trees, I was momentarily blinded by the brilliant light.

After checking the well house heater, making sure it was full of fuel and working properly so the water wouldn't freeze in the holding tank and pipes, I went back up the road and down the driveway toward the barn. Stately trees, a hundred and fifty years old or more, surrounded the barn and lined the driveway down to it. I imagined the trees were alive and able to move but stood still while I was passing. Then, when I walked away, they shook snow from their needled boughs, and danced in the moonlight, shifting the position of their branches until the next full moon appeared. A fanciful thought for a magical evening.

The light shining out in the middle of the field seemed to be coming from a heavenly door someone had left open. Moonbeams played between the outlines of the trees. Branches and brush made comical figures in the brightness. I stood in the silence breathing deeply, willing the luminous beauty to enter my body and mind. In those moments I joined a sacred forest trust, the moon's light reminding me of my own mysterious nature, known and acknowledged at these most unexpected times.

Our family took a moonlight trip in the truck to Miner's Ridge, the top of a mountain thirteen miles from our house. The dirt road wound its way up the side of the mountain, through deep gullies left by torrential rainstorms and mudslides. Steep drop-offs on one side of the road afforded fabulous views but great danger. I had heard the ridge was beautiful and the sights were fantastic, but after bumping along slowly for what seemed like a hundred miles, I wondered what could be worth seeing that we couldn't see from somewhere easier to reach.

The road narrowed and at the very top large rocks and boulders sat at the sides making it smaller still. We parked the truck, got out, and walked to the edge of the ridge. We could see Mt. Hood in Oregon, Mt. Adams in southern Washington, Mt. St. Helens and Mt. Rainier to the east. To the far north, the very top of Mt. Baker appeared on the horizon. Stunning specters like this normally had to be shared with the public. We had it to ourselves. The combination of the far mountains, and the wind whistling through the few trees that had survived the ravages of winter storms and summer heat made this trip glorious.

We took the same trip one winter day after a huge snowfall. Leaving just as the moon dropped onto the horizon, we followed the trail of snowmobiles that had gone before us. By the time we passed the last turn-off from the road to Miner's Ridge, there were no tracks. Tom and Katy led the way on his snowmobile, making a pathway for my vehicle. Several times they took off ahead of me, showing off in the soft, powdery snow. As we drove higher, the snow got deeper and the machines worked harder to make their way. About a hundred yards from the top, we realized if we went further with the snowmobiles, there was a chance they would get stuck and, with the deep snow, we wouldn't have the leverage to get them out. We got off and trudged to the top. Tom pushed snow with his body to make a path for Katy and me. Once again with the clear blue sky and no cloud cover, we could see all of the tall mountains in the distance. We rested on the hardened snow, the warm sun refreshing our tired bodies.

I watched as little whirlwinds of flakes twirled around us, dropped over the edge, fell, and disappeared onto the rocky mountainside. A sudden chill went through my body. We were at the top, no one else seemed to be headed in this direction, and we hadn't bothered to tell anyone where we were going. At my urging, we ate our snacks quickly and headed back down the snowy path.

As much as I liked being alone with my family on the ride to Miner's Ridge, I was relieved when we began to see other snowmobile tracks in the roadway. Katy and Tom played hide-and-seek games with me, scooting in amongst the trees, and then roaring out of their hiding place. Katy shrieked with laugher as she and her dad pulled up behind me, then rode off leaving me to toddle on down behind them, last one into the driveway but happiest to be home.

During the day I often had the lodge to myself, but I liked the solitude of our one-room cabin down the hill. We rarely rented it out and so it felt like a private place, much like the secret garden in the book by that name.

The structure sat back in the trees by the creek. A tiny porch had wood stacked alongside the doorway. The one square room, with a toilet and sink behind a small rock fireplace, had walls and floors that were pine tongue-and-groove. Large windows on two walls made the room bright and warm. Twin beds had matching bedspreads and the armchair fabric was a faded flower print. A tottery, black table stood under the window facing the field and the lampshade on the small lamp placed in one corner was brown and crinkled. The cabin had been built by Kay more than forty years before, and the wooden supports forming the foundation were slowly rotting underneath. We had considered trying to shore it up, but there were so many other maintenance issues around the ranch that it had low priority.

As part of my cabin routine, I built a fire, then opened all the bamboo blinds and settled on one of the beds, propping myself up with lots of pillows. Most days I brought a thermos of hot chocolate or tea, a china cup and a mystery to read. There were books on a shelf above the fireplace but they were paperbacks people had left through the years. Some were so brown and crumbly it would have been hard to turn the pages, but they added to the setting.

I often took the dogs with me. They stayed outside, ferreting chipmunks, moles, and other creatures from their earthly homes and chasing the cawing crows from the lower branches of the trees. They circled the cabin, never straying far from the front porch, knowing that I would soon let them in to toast by the fire.

From this point in the forest, I could see anyone passing either by foot or in a car, but unless they noticed the wisps of smoke coming from the chimney, I was invisible. An hour or two satisfied my need for seclusion from the world.

A mother and daughter once came to stay with us. They booked the cabin, my favorite place of solitude. Apparently they weren't happy there because after two hours they asked to be moved to the lodge. The next morning they came down the steps carrying their suitcases.

"I know we said we wanted to stay for a week," the mother said. "But it was too quiet. How do you stand staying here all the time?"

The daughter set her suitcase down on the floor. "We didn't get an ounce of sleep. It was dreadful. All we heard were the birds and the wind rattling the window. We decided we weren't meant for the forest."

The sounds that bothered these women: a bird's cry, a rattling window, or silence itself muffled by new falling snow, were signs of nature's presence and had a healing effect on me. On a hike through the forest or trip to the top of a mountain ridge, I was free from life's constraints. In those moments I collected energy and regained my personal focus. In the midst of nature I had found a surprising element – inner strength to live the life I had chosen in Goose Prairie.

Chapter Thirty-Five

BIG GAME NIGHT

B etween the end of summer camp and the worst snowfall of winter, a group of people from Seattle, Yakima and other neighboring areas worked on the nearby Boy Scout lodge, putting in countless volunteer hours on weekends and holidays. The properties committee chairman asked me if he could invite everyone who had donated time to the project to a "big game" dinner that would be held at the Double K. This big game was not the Super Bowl or a playoff but game food like elk, deer and bear. The committee would do all the cooking; the rest of the dinner would be potluck. It sounded fun so I agreed.

On a Saturday in mid-December people began arriving with large pots and huge pieces of meat wrapped in white butcher paper, which they left with us while they worked on the camp project at camp. I had to attend an all-day meeting in town so Tom took charge of the day.

Late that afternoon when I arrived home, the lodge was filled with people I knew and some friendly strangers. Dishes with salads and vegetables, rolls and desserts were laid out on the counter along with paper plates and napkins. People were gathered around the woodstove lifting lids, peering into pots of all sizes, and stirring thick boiling broth. Everyone was flushed so I knew that the woodstove had been going for some time and the wine was flowing freely.

The cooks put all the food out an hour later and what a feast. Elk stew, deer meat and beautiful pink Alaska Salmon. Potatoes, mashed and roasted, accompanied rich colored winter squash. Bright green beans and several sauces. After a short blessing and thanks for the abundance of the fields and the forest, all filled their plates and sat down to enjoy the culinary delights.

I tried the deer; it was a little tough. With lots of barbeque sauce it tasted like beef ribs without the fat. The elk was another matter. After tasting a tiny portion I quickly transferred it to Tom's plate. It tasted like it had been refrigerated, frozen, and then refrigerated too long. I didn't want to hurt anyone's feelings so I smiled and said polite things about the meal. Others around the three tables truly enjoyed eating their game.

Katy, who was usually the life of any party, became more and more withdrawn as the night went on. She ate a smidgen of salmon, but declined the small taste of game that she was offered. She grew more melancholy as people told hunting stories, joked about the meats, and ate heartily. I didn't pay too much attention to her. I assumed that she was tired from helping at camp and feeling over-stimulated by people being in the Double K lodge most of the day.

After dinner the conversation around the fireplace in the living room slowed as the embers falling from the burning logs grew brighter and then faded to deep red and finally black. The first guest said their goodbyes and others soon followed. We bid farewell to our guests from the front porch. The new falling snow quickly dampened the sound of the engines of trucks and snowmobiles. When we finally turned to go in after the last person left, there was a new coverlet of pristine white on the coal-dusted layer beneath. Shutting the heavy front door, I walked across the room and sat on the down-stuffed green couch to enjoy the after-party quiet. The fire was small now but provided enough light to create a shadow play on the walls of the great room. This was my favorite time of day. Dying embers, departed guests and silence.

Katy walked slowly through the dining room, past the fireplace and stood by me. I picked her up and she snuggled in my arms like a tiny child who's lost her way and is finally found. She lay quietly on my lap for a few minutes and then in a whisper against my chest said, "How can they do that?"

"Do what?"

"Eat my forest friends." Her voice was a mixture of anger and sadness.

I paused before answering, wanting to preserve the goodness and kindness she felt at this moment.

"Katy, they were not the same animals we see around our house every day. I know that any animal being killed makes you sad. But hunting has been a part of life for thousands of years. Sometimes it's the only way people can get food for their families. The people who were here tonight hunt for sport, but they also respect the animals whose meat they use for food. That's what tonight was about. They don't waste what they kill. They are respectful."

Her body moved slightly in my arms and she sighed.

"Anyway, you know that some of these animals would die in the forest during the winter for lack of food, because there are too many of them, especially the deer."

She looked up at me and studied my face as I saw the great concern on hers. After a long period of silence she spoke.

"I will never eat my forest friends and I hope those people never come and eat them here again." Her eyes narrowed and she took a deep breath.

"And I'll tell you something else, Mom. If I knew a salmon personally, I'd never eat them again either." She put her head down on my shoulder and eventually her body relaxed fully on my lap. She lay still, staring out towards the fire. As it died down, her eyes closed, she let out a long, tired breath and went to sleep.

Chapter Thirty-Six
ARTFUL COLLABORATION

An ambiguous relationship with winter created some agitation in me. The coziness of the fire against the work of getting it started and keeping it going and winter's beauty versus extreme temperatures often causing hardship were dueling partners. I loved the remoteness of our ranch and the solitude it afforded us. But flickering around that affection was the knowledge that a broken piece of machinery or the septic tank needing repair would be a disaster. Three to six feet of snow on the ground blocked the driveway up to the house and service people would be unable to reach us with their equipment in an emergency. But this agitation was a great motivator for writing. My conflicting emotions about winter stirred the creative pot and new ideas and projects rose to the top.

On mornings when the ranch was without guests, I sat at the square table in front of one of the living room's large picture windows to write. Outside nature set its stage. In the foreground low bushes peeked out of coal-dust covered snow piles, and varying sizes of fir and pine trees provided a lush green backdrop. As I watched, the sunlight slowly appeared above the far mountain ridge and shone through the firs. The snow glistened. Tiny droplets of water fell from the branches in a sparkling serenade as the sun rose higher in the sky.

Squirrels racing up and down the bird feeder, played "king of the mountain" from the platform at the top. Birds dive-bombed to shoo the squirrels away, then quickly pulled up and flew towards the snow-dusted branches above. Rabbits nosed at the ground trying to find food, then quickly disappeared or were hidden by the whiteness of their fur against the snow.

These window-framed images gave birth to the idea of writing poetry. I thought I would create poetry by choosing forms particular to certain poets, study their poems and then choose my own subject. Using that same form I would begin writing my own verses.

One cold, rainy day in late winter, I decided to use the sonnet as the basis of my writing. I took poetry books down from the shelves and began reading Shakespeare, Dunne, Milton, Keats and Wordsworth. I analyzed the structure, word usage and images they had created in their writing. Now it was my turn to attempt to write a sonnet.

I watched out the window to contemplate the landscape. The crows and Canada Jays in the trees, with their feathers fluffed up around them, sat staring out from the branches that sheltered them from the heaviest rain. Occasionally the crow would sound an alarm, to whom or for what reason I would never know, but it was loud and eerie. The sky was the color of dark iron and clouds moved quickly over the trees, creating patterns in gray and white that changed each time I looked up. As the rain continued, the firs' branches sagged under the weight of the water-laden snow. Through an opening in the trees I saw the field by the barn. The elk, single file, moved silently into the forest's edge and disappeared. Indentations where they had lain were barely visible in the field below. I could see rabbit tracks going in different directions, to and from patches of frozen grass where the snow had been washed away by the rain.

On the cusp of spring's arrival winter hung on like a bothersome relative visiting for weeks. In those moments of suspended time, I longed for the sun, blue sky and the delicate surprises of spring's wildflower bloom. Just as the final signs of winter were so obvious, now the hints of spring seemed to come into view. In the sky to the southwest the clouds were breaking up. A squirrel scurried up a post and stood on the fence, letting out a great squeal as if to call the forest creatures from their hiding places. The rain caused the snow to fall from the trees and their branches were once again able to straighten and breathe. I felt a surge of hope. We were going to make it through this winter. Spring would soon arrive in its many-faceted splendor bringing renewed energy for life at Goose Prairie.

For the next several hours I played with words, sounds, length of line, and put the impressions of the time spent looking out the window into sonnet form. It may never win a prize, but each reading fills me with memories of that day when the masters of the past, signs of winter's departure and this novice poet, came together and spent the day in artful collaboration.

WINTER SONNET

I hear the rooftop cadence of the rain,
Cackling from its branch, the fluffed feathered crow,
See languishing firs ladened with drenched snow,
Outlines in the field of white where elk have lain.
Varied tracks of rabbits show whence they came
And back again crisscrossing to and fro.
The somber jay sings his adagio,
Cold's melancholy mantle shrouds this terrain.

In the southwest sky flecks of blue appear.
Beyond the fence a squirrel chirrups his jeer.
Winter's hand loosens its icy hold
As Lilliputian signs of spring unfold.
Waiting ones, longing for a blaze of sun,
Awake! Wearisome winter's almost done!

Chapter Thirty-Seven

JUST AROUND THE CORNER

During late February each year were two weeks when the temperature rose and the sun shone more brightly. The lengthening of daylight hours gave us hope that spring was going to arrive full-blown in the near future. The snow began to disappear off the hillsides. As the snow melted in patterns from the trunk outward pale greens and brown appeared. It would no doubt snow again before spring was officially declared, but the ground was warming and even a deep snow's stay would now be minimal. During these few weeks the forest beckoned us to come and enjoy its emergence from winter.

On a Saturday during this warm streak, Katy and I went for a climb on the mountain behind the lodge. I loved hiking with Katy. Her focused attitude on the smallest detail of nature and her seven-year old enthusiasm delighted me and helped hone my own senses and perception of the natural world. I was concerned about getting directionally confused, but Tom assured me that as long as we didn't cross the ridge and go down the other side, we could come straight down our side and eventually reach the road and hike home from that point.

Early in the afternoon with the sun's warm light surrounding us and lulling us into a somewhat euphoric state, we started out, wearing light coats, medium pants, and heavy hiking boots. We took a snack packed in a plastic bag and brought Samantha and Bear who always loved a forest outing.

Although there was still snow on the mountainside, we were able to navigate our way around trees, stumps, and forest floor rubble. After hiking straight up a man-made trail for a quarter mile, we began to zigzag, following the switchback trails that elk, bear, and deer had stomped out over the year. I made mental notes of odd-shaped bushes, unusual tree formations and clearings that might serve as markers on our way back.

We talked and laughed as we made our way up the mountain. The underbrush was getting thicker, the terrain steeper and the debris from winter storms denser as we climbed. The dogs ran in front, circling around and occasionally barking as if encouraging us to keep walking at a good pace. The warmth and light from the sun seemed to intensify as we got higher, and, after two hours of steady hiking, we saw the mountain peaks across the valley. A clearing, with a view out over the trees, provided a lovely, serene place to rest. We sat on the ground, dried pine needles providing a warm, cushioned pillow beneath our bodies.

"Bring on the snack!"

"Here," Katy said as she passed a stack pack of soda crackers, some bread, a banana, and a small cardboard juice container to me. "All my favorite things!"

Carbohydrates. She was nicknamed the "carbo-queen" and that was her diet. We chuckled about it as we sat enjoying the warmth that held great promise after the snow and cold rain of November, December and January. The forest's whispering silence intermingled with the rustle of leaves and calls of the birds. Samantha and Bear went from squirrel hole to broken branch, to animal droppings, sniffing madly, rolling in bear or cougar scat, and then dashing to something else of interest. I felt my thoughts lighten and my body relax as I watched their joyous exploration.

They slowed their pace, stopped, and found a warm place to lie down, their legs stiffening in a languid stretch then relaxing as they napped in the cool mountain air. The duet of sound and silence gave me a sense of satisfaction with life and delight with the trees, bushes and birds surrounding our mountain retreat.

Katy played nearby, quietly talking to herself as she made up conversations with the birds and trees. She pretended to track animals on the forest floor, touched tender new growth with gentleness, and explored the area around stumps and logs in the vicinity of our pine needle couch. I closed my eyes, relaxed even more and would have drifted off to sleep if a sudden chill in the soft breeze had not roused me from my lethargic state. I sat up and realized the sun was moving closer to the ridge of the mountain across the valley and its light would soon be blocked from our mountainside.

I gathered leftover crackers, banana peels, and juice containers, put them into the plastic bag, and called Katy and the dogs who were playing together at the edge of the clearing. The dogs stood motionless as Katy and I paused, taking in the scent of the pines, the chirping of the Canada Jays, and the light playing off the melting snow mounds around us.

"Goodbye, beautiful mountain. Goodbye big trees. Goodbye little birds."

Katy's soft-spoken farewell was the perfect coda to an afternoon of nature's symphony of sights, smells, and sounds. Heading down the animal trails, I looked for the marks that were so obvious on the way up the mountain, but now seemed non-existent. The trees, pathways and clearings didn't bear any resemblance to what I remembered.

"Your dad says that all we have to do is keep walking down and we'll come out on the road somewhere." Who was I trying to reassure here? "Let's try and walk a little faster, Katy. It's going to be harder to get to the road if it's dark."

We walked at a faster pace, occasionally stumbling on a branch or stepping in a hole covered by snow and decaying leaves, tripping and falling forward, making the downward journey more difficult than the climb up. Several times we stopped at intersections of elk trails, and I thought I recognized a landmark. But, the further along we went the more my dismay grew. It was important not to alarm Katy, but I was beginning to think we were lost. Going up we had zigzagged equally to the left and right, so our trip would be fairly straight up, but now I had my doubts about my hiking methodology.

The dogs followed behind, tired from the circles they had run around us chasing squirrels and birds. Once again I urged Katy to walk faster. She wanted to look at animal tracks and fallen tree branches as we walked down the mountain but the thought of us being alone in the forest at night with lightweight clothing and the company of bears and cougar was not my idea of a positive end to a wonderful day. She sensed my anxiety and offered encouragement.

"I recognize these trails, Mom. We're doing just fine."

What does a seven-year-old know? I played along with her confident manner as we walked briskly, singing songs, telling jokes to each other, and talking about what she had seen in her observations around the clearing. The sky's blue color was beginning to fade to grey and I knew if we didn't get home soon it would be extremely difficult to tell what direction we were headed. The sun sank below the ridge and the sky darkened further.

"I see the barn!" Katy was gleeful and excited. "That's the metal roof!"

"No, honey, it can't be. I don't see anything."

"I do! It's our barn. I recognize the roof!"

I didn't see anything as I scanned the trees, but in a few minutes we came out into a clearing. There was our barn, about a hundred feet in front of us! The dogs ran ahead yipping and getting in each other's way as they headed up the lane. Relief and weariness came over me as we trudged over the snow towards the lodge and the light from the kitchen window. Tom was waiting at the door, concern on his face. Katy ran the last few yards to him, and he gathered her up in his arms.

"So, how was the forest today?"

Her words tumbled over each other as she told her dad all about the dogs, the animal trails and the beautiful clearing far up the hill. She whispered that I had been worried about the dark, and that she saved the day when she saw the barn. It was a conspiratorial conversation, the two mountain people laughing at the city mama. I removed my coat and wet boots, went to the living room and sank into a soft overstuffed chair by the fire. Katy chattered away to Tom as they made tea to warm us up.

The dogs walked into the room, circled, and plopped down in front of the fireplace. Samantha stared into the fire for a few moments and her head dropped to the floor. Bear came to lie at my feet. I rubbed her ears and stroked her back. She looked up and I smiled remembering what a great day we'd had.

Chapter Thirty-Eight

BASEMENT DELIGHTS

There were little creatures down in the basement. I knew they were there, waiting for me to go back upstairs before they resumed scurrying around, doing whatever basement creatures do. I had captured enough little mouse bodies in those snap traps to know that they existed. Kay and Isabelle had left the heavy back doors open each summer they had lived in the house, so I was sure mouse residency had been established in quiet corners, under loose boards and behind ten pound lumps of coal many generations ago.

Fresh vegetables, melons and other fruits were stored on top of an old, wooden door suspended from the rafters by four long wires. It kept the small creatures from gnawing at the produce. Canned fruits and vegetables, paper goods and cleaning supplies lined shelves along another wall while an aged propane gas refrigerator stood guard in the corner near the cleaning supplies.

Whenever I ventured down the opened-back stairway to the basement to get a melon or a bag of carrots, I took a deep breath and went quickly. There was a gaslight near the bottom, but if I were only going to be there for a minute, I didn't bother lighting it. I grabbed what I needed and went back up the stairs, hoping I wouldn't step on any little mouse, run into a packrat, hear strange noises from the coal pile in the far corner or feel something trying to snag my legs through the openings on the steps. Out came my breath in a sigh of relief as I closed the door and congratulated myself on another successful trip to the basement without incident.

One Saturday morning I made my quick trip down the basement stairs, started back up and realized I had forgotten to get a honeydew melon off the swinging door shelf. There were half a dozen in a divided box. I couldn't see them clearly, but I reached my hand into the box and jerked it out. Sticky liquid and squishy, strings of fruit pulp dripped from my fingers. I put my hand back in and felt around. The top of the melon was missing and my hand was swimming in fruit and juice. I reached for the next one in the box, presuming that the first melon had over ripened and split. The second one was the same. Pulling my hand out of the box, I went to the laundry tub to wash the melon juice off before lighting the lamp.

As the soft gaslight glow grew brighter, the destruction in the box became evident. The top of each melon had been gnawed off. The rest of the melon was intact. Six, gorgeous, delicious melons meant for a week's worth of guests' breakfasts were destroyed. I didn't mind sharing the melons with the animals, but why did they have to eat through all of them?

I searched the basement for the culprit but only found bits of melon rind here and there. A Hansel and Gretel pathway would have made the search more satisfying. This had been a quiet and sneaky thief, like a squirrel or a packrat.

After the melon incident, the fly population increased. Even though I cleaned the juice and melon parts off the hanging door and the dirt floor below it, a sweet smell lingered on the unfinished door. The juice had had plenty of time to permeate the wood and make it a fabulous resting place for flies. I asked Tom to spray or figure out some way to get rid of the flies hovering around the vegetables and fruit. He said he would take care of it.

One day before dawn I made my way down the stairs. In a hurry, I was gathering what I needed to begin breakfast for a large group arriving early that morning. Moving quickly from the canned goods to the paper products, I darted over to get some produce. I picked up some oranges and turned to head back upstairs when something grabbed my hair. I turned in the other direction, dropping the oranges onto the shelf and felt the same thing flying into the opposite side of my face. I screamed, dropping the rest of the groceries on the floor, and tried to get the attacker out of my hair. It was hanging from the rafters and wouldn't let go. I put my hands up, trying to push it away and my hands stuck to it as well. Fly paper! I was stuck to flypaper.

"What's all the screaming? Are you okay?"

Tom was on his way down the stairs with a flashlight. He shone it in my direction, stopped, looked at my face and burst out laughing. I had strips of flypaper complete with little dead fly bodies stuck on my hair in three places.

"Get it off of me. How am I going to get this out of my hair?" It was disgusting.

"Stand still. Let me see what I can do." He put the flashlight under his arm and came down the stairs the rest of the way. I started to laugh and cry at the same time. He pulled on one piece of the paper strip and flies flipped around and landed in my face and clothing.

"Oh my gosh. Stop! Get them out of my hair. This is so icky."

"Hold still, hold still. You're making it worse by moving."

"Ouch! You're hurting me. My hair is coming off on the flypaper." I had lots of hair to spare, but having it pulled out was not enjoyable.

"Make up your mind," he said. "Do you want them out or not?" His hands were beginning to get entangled with the fly strips. "I think we'll have to cut them out."

He was trying not to laugh, but holding the flashlight, flicking flies out of his wife's hair, and trying to get sticky paper to release its grip got the best of him.

"Come upstairs. We'll see what we can do." So back up the stairs I went looking like Medusa with writhing snakes of flypaper hair. A combination of cutting, peanut butter and patience left me looking as good as new. Tom was somewhat penitent about the placement of the flypaper, amused at the early morning entertainment I had provided, and very careful about where he put the replacements.

The washing machine and dryer located in the basement needed electricity to operate. What a wonderful thing that was. While doing laundry, I could have the lights on. That meant that the little creatures, both flying and scurrying, stayed out of view. When the lights were on, the basement seemed almost normal. It was cool in the summer and warm in the winter and when the dryer was going it was quite cozy.

Katy liked to be in the basement with me. She had her finger paints and an easel Tom built for her and she liked having a place where she could be as messy as she wanted and I wouldn't fuss about it. Several times Katy asked to have a bath in the laundry tub. Since her body was so little at age six, I obliged. First she painted, getting more on herself than on the paper and then, with the help of a chair, climbed into the deep, square, concrete sink, which I had heated with boiling water and let cool. She treated it like a hot tub or spa treatment giving a great sigh of enjoyment, her eyes closing, head leaning on the edge, body relaxing into the water. At the end of her soaking time, I scrubbed her back, lifted her out of the water and wrapped her in a large, thick, oversized towel I had heated in the dryer as she was bathing. I carried her up the steps, into the apartment and left her with Tom for the rest of the bedtime routine.

One particular night, I went back down to the basement to finish getting the laundry out of the dryer. I stood in the quiet, folding sheets and towels, savoring the solitude after all the activity with Katy. Suddenly from behind the washing machine I heard a scraping sound like someone pulling metal over rocks. It stopped and started again. I stood there trying to identify its exact location. It kept moving but now sounded like a rake on gravel. Whatever was making the sound was traveling away from the washing machine, which stood on a concrete slab, and towards the shelves, which were built above the dirt and gravel floor.

I grabbed the flashlight and walked along the wall looking for the noisemaker and listening for the sound. About five feet from the end of the concrete slab, a large packrat was dragging itself forward, its back foot caught in a mousetrap. As the light shone on the animal, it started moving faster. I knew that I didn't want packrats in my basement, but I also didn't want to mangle them either.

Yelling for Tom to come down to the basement, I watched the poor little fellow's progress.

"What's going on down here?"

"Look. There's a packrat pulling himself along the wall and he's got a trap caught on his back leg."

We watched the packrat pull himself step by step for a few more feet and then Tom said, "We've got to kill him. We can't let him die a slow death here in the basement and he *will* die."

I stood in silence, watching the packrat. He was getting slower and his movement more labored, or that's what I wanted to believe.

"How will we do it?" We? I wasn't going to do it, whatever *it* was. I was paralyzed by the thought of having to kill an animal. I saw the packrat stop to rest, his breath taken in gasps now. I looked at Tom and he at me.

"Go on upstairs. I'll take care of it." He didn't like it any better than I did, but he was willing to take responsibility for destroying the wounded animal. I tried not to cry as I went up the steps because I knew that would make Tom feel even worse. But in the kitchen I sobbed, trying not to let the sound escape from my throat. Tom would know from my red eyes and inability to speak that I had been crying, but at least he wouldn't have to witness it. He came up the stairs a few minutes later with the packrat wrapped in newspaper. After putting it in a bag, he carried it to the apartment.

"I'll go turn off the generator," he said and went out the back door with the bag.

Going back to the kitchen, I shut the basement door and waited for the electricity to go out. I fixed two cups of tea, turned the gaslight off and went to greet Tom, who came in the door without the bag. How often he responded to my inability to act, handling it without complaining, but, I'm sure, with as much sadness as I felt. I gave him the tea and a hug, a small token of my gratitude for taking care of something I could not handle.

Kay and Isabelle gave us winter instructions for the huge coal furnace in the basement. We knew about cleaning out the pipe leading to the chimney. That was a job that created its own mess. The pipe filled with soot rapidly and had to be cleaned out at least monthly. The black powder poured out, blew everywhere and left us looking like Dick Van Dyke in "Mary Poppins." No matter how hard we tried to clean our shoes they left a trail of black prints across the linoleum kitchen floor for a day or two. When the furnace was not used during the summer, it brought a few months' respite. What Kay and Isabelle had not given us were instructions for the summer's shutdown.

In the lodge great room, there was a two by two foot grate. During the winter the cold air entered from two intake openings at the sides of the furnace and forced the hot air up into the great room and eventually to the rest of the house. The system was fairly ingenious since it didn't require any electricity to operate. We weren't really sure of how it worked. We assumed that when the fire was out for the summer, the furnace was sealed off from the upstairs rooms and we didn't have to leave the doors to the fire box in the basement closed. How wrong we were! Through the firebox door, little basement creatures tried to invade the upper floor.

On nights when the moon was full and the forest was alive with bird and animal noises, I had trouble sleeping, not from the sounds, but from the energy-charged atmosphere. Not wanting to disturb Tom with my sleepless agitation, I moved to the down-filled couch in the great room when we didn't have guests. It was inviting and enveloped me in warmth and comfort. The large grate that opened to the furnace below was at the end of the couch where I had my pillow. Each time I slept there, I was awakened by a faint, scratching noise. Nothing to be particularly alarmed at, but annoying when one is trying to fall asleep.

When I slept in the great room over the summer, the noise increased until finally one night, I got up and tracked the sound. The moon provided enough light for a quick search in corners, behind furniture and even across the beams of the ceiling. As I walked, the scratching stopped.

I lay down again and a minute later the noise returned. I grabbed the flashlight from the desk and scanned the room with the light. There wasn't anything moving. The scratching stopped. Standing very still, I was ready to shine the flashlight whenever the sound started again. In a few seconds I heard the tiny noise, which now seemed deafening in the silence of the room. It was coming from the furnace grate in the floor.

I shone the light inside the grate. What seemed like hundreds of mice, scurried back and forth in the space about five feet below, on top of the furnace. Their little beady eyes looked at the beam of light and then looked elsewhere. They weren't even afraid of my standing there. I could see nutshells, little pieces of breadcrumbs and other items I didn't recognize strewn about the metal top. It looked like a picnic ground.

Something had to be done about this before winter or the lodge would be overrun during the cold season when the field mice swarmed in wanting to set up quarters in the basement beside the permanent mice residents. That morning, I lifted the grate and dropped two boxes of mouse killer pellets onto the top of the furnace. Within days, the scratching sound had ceased. Most had gone, but many had died on top of the grate. I had to get rid of them before we started the furnace for the winter or the smell would drive us out of the building.

Tom suggested that we use the shop vacuum to pick them up. Good idea, except that neither of us had arms long enough to reach down the grate with the nozzle and get the mice. But we did have a little girl, who didn't weigh very much. With an idea in mind we approached Katy who was excited by the prospect of this adventure. Her only stipulation was that when we were done we had to count the mice. We agreed.

Holding her by her legs, Tom lowered her upside down into the furnace pipe, which was very wide, with the vacuum nozzle in her hand,. She vacuumed the top and reached as far down the sides of the furnace as her arms would reach. Tom hauled her back up and we counted the mice in the bottom of the shop vacuum. She was thrilled: she had vacuumed up twenty four. The furnace door was closed from then on and the mouse picnic ground was closed for good.

Chapter Thirty-Nine

ADVENTURE IN COAL

T he red coal truck huffed and puffed its way up the driveway looking and sounding like "the little engine that could". The ground was soaked and layers of soggy leaves made it slippery and bouncy like a Scottish bog. The delivery was late, light was fading fast.

The driver, who had delivered coal to us for four years and to Kay and Isabelle for many previous years, pulled the truck up to the front of the house, slid out from the front seat and dropped to the ground.

"Here," he spoke gruffly as he handed me a clipboard covered with coal dust. "Sign this. Where's it going? Same place?"

"Same place," I replied, trying to hold back on an incredulous look. He had delivered the first five tons just a few days before. Where else would we put the coal? "The ground is very wet and I've brought some plywood for you to drive over in the yard."

"I don't need any plywood. The ground will be fine."

"Are you sure? I don't want the truck stuck here for the winter."

I chuckled at my little joke. He looked at me with distain.

"I've been delivering this stuff here for a long time and I know when I'll get stuck and when I won't."

He harrumphed, climbed back into the cab of the truck and began to back into the space between the front porch and a huge stump. Inching backward, he tried to line the truck up with the coal window in the basement wall. The truck was off by several feet, so he drove forward. The wheels slipped on the sloppy ground and grabbed hold. The coal-ladened truck lurched forward several yards and stopped. The driver ground the gears into reverse one more time and backed up. The truck stopped. The driver jumped out, and began to lower the coal shoot from the back of the truck, grumbling under his breath just loud enough for me to hear.

"Damn, this still isn't right. I'll have to move the truck again."

I nodded, not wanting to commit myself to a comment that might set him off.

He climbed back into the truck and started the engine. I heard him shift into first gear. The wheels spun. The truck didn't move. He tried again and the wheels made holes in the front grassy area. He threw the gears into reverse. The wheels dug deeper. He began to rock the truck, forward, reverse, forward, reverse. But the truck was stuck. He got out and began to lower the coal shoot one more time.

"What are you doing?" He wasn't even close to the basement window.

"Look, lady, I've got to dump the load here so I can get my truck out. The truck will be lighter and I'll be able to move it. I've got to get back to Yakima."

"But you've got to put it into the basement. That's five tons of coal. What are we supposed to do? Shovel it in there?"

"I don't care how you get it in there. I've got to move and I can't get any closer to the window with the coal in the truck." Without another word, he began to let the coal drop down the shoot on the grass.

The coal dust flew everywhere. I went into the house to escape the black mess. No wonder his skin, clothes and demeanor were so dark. Soon the crashing sound of the coal dropping stopped and the sound of wheels, aimlessly spinning, could be heard. I headed out the front door and yelled to the driver.

"Stop. You're making huge holes. You should have put the wood down like I asked." His lips moved, probably saying words I didn't want to hear. He sat in his truck, then climbed down again and looked at the back wheels. They were about halfway into the ground and the front ones were sitting up high. Maybe the truck would be in our front yard all winter. Better the truck than the driver.

"I'll have to call my boss. Where's your phone?"

"We don't have regular phones up here. We'll have to see if we can get through on the radio phone." His rudeness made me want to ask him to walk to Whistlin' Jack to make the phone call. Looking at the coal dumped in the yard made me want to weep.

"Come on in. We'll see if we can reach someone."

He finally got through to the fuel company office. I heard him arguing with the person on the other end of the line, denying what I knew to be true. He *hadn't* taken the necessary precautions before backing the truck up.

"They're sending a tow truck up right away. Take them about an hour." He went to the back door and paused. I looked at him but didn't invite him to stay inside. Where would he sit in those grimy clothes? And, more importantly, why have this nasty person in my house any more than necessary? He opened the door and went out into the rain. I sat in the apartment waiting for Tom to come home.

The tow truck and Tom arrived at the same time. I watched while the tow truck driver, whose shirt had "Ed" embroidered on his shirt, and the coal man argued about getting the coal vehicle unstuck.

Ed walked away, got into the tow truck, turned it around and shone a huge spotlight on the muddy mess. He pulled out a long bulky chain, with a hook at the end, ran it around one of the broadest trees by the driveway, and attached it to the bumper of the coal truck. I was disturbed they were not thinking about the consequences for the tree. I yelled to Ed.

"You're going to kill the tree by doing this."

"Nah, we've done this before. It's not going to kill it."

Maim, ruin, break or deform, but not kill. I didn't pursue the matter. I wanted the coal truck gone from the front of the house. I wanted the grimy coal man off the property.

Tom joined me on the porch to watch the spectacle. Ed began moving his vehicle slowly down the driveway. The chain tightened. The coal truck didn't move immediately, but the tree looked like it was bending slightly toward the house. Ed again inched along and finally the coal truck started to move forward. Muddy water and rock flew from under its wheels spattering everything close by. Ed kept his vehicle moving until the coal truck had its front wheels on the gravel driveway and the back wheels were out of the trenches it had dug. He got out, undid the chain and drove off down the drive, slowing at the bottom to be sure the coal man was following.

"They leave, and we're left with one big mess." In front of us were two huge holes and five tons of coal. What had been the last remnants of summer's wildflowers and autumn's red and gold hues now was black spattered brown and ugly.

We went to the Goose Prairie Inn for dinner. Katy had been playing in the store with the owners' grandchildren. Several of the other prairie residents were there and we told the story of the great coal adventure.

"Our biggest concern is the rain, and getting the coal into the basement. I'll probably be shoveling for the rest of the year." I knew I would have to do most of it since Tom had to go to work each day.

"When are you going to begin shoveling it? I'll be glad to help." Webb was always ready to help neighbors.

Another one of our good friends, Dick spoke up as well. "Sure, we'll all come and give you a hand. Just tell us when." We decided the next afternoon would be best for everyone. Tom would pick up Katy and we'd begin.

It was raining the next day. Everyone showed up in heavy rain gear and boots, carrying shovels of all sizes. We began heaving large pieces of coal into the basement window and shoveling the smaller ones underneath. As it got darker, I turned on the generator so we could work by the lights on the porch. Our raingear was covered with black dust, our faces streaked with dark lines, and our hands almost solidly black. Just like the coal man!

When the last bits of coal had been cleared from the yard, I invited our neighbors in. Everyone declined wanting to go home and shower. Me, too. Tom and I thanked them profusely as they walked down the driveway blending quickly into the darkness with their blackened clothing.

I went to the garage, shut off the generator and headed to the house. Tom met me at the door and told me to take the raingear off outside. He grabbed it and went down the basement stairs. I followed. In the light of the gas lamps, I saw how black the clothing was. We tried to wash it in the sink, but the coal dust stuck like confectionary sugar on toast. Nothing seemed to get it off.

"Guess that's it for these clothes." I wasn't going to spend days trying to clean them nor were they going in the washing machine.

I am amazed that what I remember most about Goose Prairie is the hard times, made easier by practical friendship and *doing* rather than talking. Normally, the waste of clothing would have upset me. But the generosity, humor, and the good nature of our neighbors helped me feel satisfied with the situation. We had fun together. But what made the fun memorable was the help I received without asking given by neighbors always alert to need.

Chapter Forty

THANKSGIVING FINALE

Our last Thanksgiving at the Prairie was an extra special time. We believed it would be our final one at the Double K lodge. Tom and I put the lodge and property on the market and were negotiating with some people from Seattle. Snow had fallen in the previous weeks. Although it created problems arriving so early, it was a beautiful blanket over the dead leaves and debris that lay in the dormant forest.

Before Tom's immediate family arrived, mounds of snow had fallen from the steeply pitched roof, blocking most of the drive beside the house. Their car could still make it up to the front of the house. We were pleased there was enough snow for the cousins to ski but not so much that we couldn't get in and out of Goose Prairie. And the snow pack was deep enough for us to ride the snowmobiles for the first time that season.

The day after Thanksgiving, Tom and I took turns taking each of the relatives out on the snowmobiles. None had any experience with snowmobiles. The procedure was fairly simple. Each of the teenage cousins took a ride first. Tom led them along the road, down to the lake and back, they using my slower but more predictable machine and Tom his own. We finally convinced Tom's older brother, David, to put on a snowsuit and go. He did seem to enjoy it but was happy to have both feet on the ground again.

Then it was Tom's younger brother Ken's turn. Tom suggested that I lead the way this time, and, at my urging, Ken reluctantly took Tom's snow machine. We rode down the drive and turned on to the road. The weather was beginning to change. The sky was filling with low-lying storm clouds. We went at a leisurely pace while Ken got used to the machine; then we played games of speeding past each other and waiting for the other to catch up. The road was absolutely clear, not a car or another snowmobile anywhere. I relaxed and truly enjoyed my ride.

It was exhilarating sitting on the snowmobile experiencing all the power that the machine delivered. I felt the mechanical energy of the snowmobile contained in my body. The speed, combined with the raw elements of the weather and the isolation of the forest, forced all thoughts of mortality aside. I felt brave and invincible that day.

Ken and I rode to the lake. Because the road was clear and the wind whirled around enticing us with its winter dance, we decided to go on into the forest along the mountain road. The clouds were getting lower. The snow began to fall more heavily as we ascended the mountain via the road. I zoomed ahead of Ken. About a mile ahead I switched off the snowmobile to enjoy the stillness of the forest. The engine noise from the other snowmobile was a tiny muffled sound in the distance. The blanket of snow covering trees and brush provided thick insulation from the sound. Shortly, Ken appeared and guided his snowmobile around beside mine.

"How about a couple more miles up?" I asked. He looked at the sky and the ground around us.

"No. We should head home."

I was surprised. I'm the cautious one in dangerous situations. I was feeling the confidence to do miles and miles even in the most treacherous weather. I relented reluctantly.

We turned the snowmobiles around and at a steady pace headed down the mountain. The snow was now more than two feet deep, swirling in huge gusts around each turn in the road and falling so fast that it became difficult to see very far. The tracks were still visible from our trip up the mountain, but in a few hours no one would know we had traveled there. Passing the lake, we were soon on the paved portion of the road again. The snowfall was less heavy at this altitude but still coming down steadily.

Following the road we kept together at a moderate speed, rode past the camp signs, the Goose Prairie Inn, turned at the driveway and rode up to the house. We parked the snowmobiles in the drive beside the living room windows and put plastic covers over them to protect from the falling snow. We never would have guessed that this would be the last time they would be ridden by any of the family.

That evening the snow turned to rain and during the night it began to snow again, snowing all night and into the morning. We drove with the family as far as Squaw Rock and said our good-byes. Tom, Katy and I drove back to the Prairie. The snow on the road was becoming much deeper as we passed the 3000-feet elevation marker.

At home the snow had fallen off of the roof onto the snowmobiles and only the handgrips were visible. We decided that as soon as the snow stopped, we would dig them out and move them to their usual spot outside of the apartment where the snow stayed on the roof most of the winter.

The afternoon precipitation changed again and again – rain, then snow and then back to rain as the temperature fluctuated on each side of the freezing point. About seven p.m. the snow stopped, the sky cleared and the temperature dropped into the teens. The snowmobiles were no longer visible. With the temperature so low we knew that we wouldn't be riding. We decided to wait until the next weekend to dig them out.

At midweek, the temperatures rose in the evening. During the night, we heard a terrible rumbling sound and a grinding crash several times. Then it was quiet. Going to the windows, I looked for the source of the noise but didn't see anything out of the ordinary and I presumed that some branches, under the weight of the snow, had broken off a tree and hit either the generator house or the barn.

That morning when Katy and Tom left for school and work, it was still dark. In the reflection of the gaslight, we didn't see anything different in front of the house or near the kitchen. But when dawn came and the light worked its way around the corner to the side of the living room, I saw the cause of the midnight rumbling crash. Huge pieces of ice, half a foot thick and as big as quarter sheets of plywood, had loosened from the metal roof and crashed onto the ground below. Our snowmobiles were now under five feet of snow and enormous pieces of ice. Over the next several days, the warming by day and freezing temperatures at night caused the ice to melt and refreeze, forming an impenetrable fortress around the snowmobiles. No amount of chipping with a shovel would free the machines and because we were unsure of their exact location under the mass of ice and snow we were reluctant to use a pickax or sledgehammer. All we could do now was hope for a few days of warmer weather to soften the outside of the icy mass. That was a hope abandoned in the following weeks. The snow continued throughout December and into January.

Chapter Forty-One

NOT SO SUPER SUNDAY

In January the snow melted during the day and at night, froze again when temperatures dropped. Water overflowed from the creek diversion pipes at the bottom of the driveway and created ice blocks on the sides. The drive through the creek was hazardous. Clearing the driveway of heavy wet snow was a useless endeavor. During the day we walked in the slush; at night we slid into and around the frozen indentations of the day's footprints.

On Super Bowl Sunday 1995, we were invited to a party at Denny and Darlene's house, which we had been looking forward to since Christmas. In winter all of us tended to stay close to home. With the Inn was closed for the winter, we missed having that daily coffee gathering with prairie friends.

Tom insisted on clearing the drive with the snow blower before we went to the party. What foolishness, I thought. It would only fill with snow again. But nothing I said would stop the actions of a stubborn man intent on fighting Mother Nature. He bundled up, went outside, and eventually I heard the snow blower go past the back door.

The generator was on. I was doing laundry in the basement, running up and down the stairs and hanging up clothes. I occasionally stopped by the picture windows to assess the amount of drizzle falling on the coal-dust blackened snow outside. The air's heaviness muffled the sounds from the forest.

I stuck my head out the door. An odd sounding birdcall filtered through the trees. It wasn't a typical call, but faint and different each time. Why was the forest so quiet except for that sound? I called Katy from the apartment to come and listen.

"What's so different about that bird sound, Kates?"

She pushed past outside. Standing on the porch, she listened intently.

"I think it's someone yelling. Did Dad come in? I don't hear the snow blower. Do you?"

"Oh my, Katy. Something's wrong!" We ran to the apartment and yanked on boots, coats, gloves and hats. With the dogs following (hoping for the next great adventure) we ran down the driveway calling for Tom. About halfway between the bottom of the drive and the main road, Tom lay sprawled on the ground looking cold and soaked from the wet snow. He had stumbled on ice and his leg had slipped under the snow blower. He couldn't bend his leg without considerable pain.

"Are you bleeding? Can you walk at all? How long have you been lying here?"

"I don't know. I've been crawling along in the snow trying to get closer to the house. I don't see any blood. Get the car and bring it down. We need to go the emergency room now." I ran to the house, grabbed the keys, and drove the car down the drive over the ice mounds. I pulled slowly up next to him.

As Katy and I tried to lift him, his leg bent and he cried out in pain. Katy opened the car's back door as wide as possible. We wanted to put Tom in the back to rest his leg on the seat. But the back door didn't open wide enough so we pushed the front seat all the way back, reclined it, and rested him on the front seat. Katy and I had done all we could. Tom had to get himself turned around and facing forward on the seat, bending his leg and pulling it into the car. That was excruciating for all of us. I drove the car to the house for dry clothing, blankets, and a pillow to protect his leg on the trip to town.

As I drove down the slushy, icy road, Katy sat in back and tried to sooth her father. Where did it hurt most? Was it warm enough? Did he want the blanket up closer to his chin? How comfortable was his seat? Did he want her to rub his head to make him feel better? He assured her he was comfortable. What a sweet liar he was.

At the emergency room in Yakima an hour later we got him out of the car and into a wheelchair with his leg extended. The nurse wheeled him into the examining room, x-rayed his knee and asked which orthopedic surgeon to call. Without hesitating, Tom asked for Dr. John Place, a man who was active in scouting, an excellent doctor, and a person Tom admired and trusted.

John, dressed in sweats, arrived a short time later and clipped the x-rays to the light box over Tom's gurney as he examined Tom's leg. He teased Tom about taking him away from the Super Bowl (he said he had made Tom wait until halftime), talked about an upcoming canoe trip, and asked him questions about the winter campout in February.

I was relieved to have someone else in the room with us as I contemplated all the things I had to do in the next few days. We had a group of guests arriving for the weekend and I needed to prepare food and clean for them. The laundry was waiting to be picked up and I was scheduled to work at Katy's school later in the week. I believed Tom would be laid up for a week or so with what I thought was a twisted muscle or a dislocated joint.

The x-rays told a different story. Tom's kneecap was detached and sitting about four inches up on his thigh. Surgery would be necessary and Dr. Place would do it the next day. But there were no rooms available at the hospital Sunday night so I had to take Tom to a local motel until morning. He was given medication to make him comfortable and I hoped it would kick in before he had to bend his leg again.

Katy was thrilled to stay in town at a hotel with lights, heat, and best of all television. I bought dinner for them, but I couldn't eat. Anxiety took hold. I thought of what this was going to mean over the next few weeks. Tom could no longer help at the lodge. We wouldn't be able to stay there because I couldn't transport him over snow into the building. And I had no way to carry him back out to the car for each visit to the doctor, the physical therapist or anywhere else. He couldn't be left alone for any length of time because he couldn't walk.

At nine p.m. I drove to the lodge, built up the fires for the night, got the guest list for the coming weekend and loaded the dogs into the car. Fortunately, the temperatures were not predicted in the subzero range for the coming week. The pipes wouldn't freeze in the next few days. After a fitful night, I delivered Tom to the hospital the next morning and took Katy to school.

After the surgery, Dr. Place said Tom would be released the next afternoon. I had expected the hospital to keep him until he stabilized. This meant I would have to transport him somewhere, keep him there for two or three weeks until he began therapy, and drive him to the sessions in town. How could I do this from Goose Prairie where bumping over ice and snow cover would endanger the work done on his knee? So a motel halfway between the ranch and Katy's school became our home for a week while I looked for a more permanent location to house us all.

The small rented motel cabin was barely adequate for the care I needed to give Tom. It was dark, damp, and the beds were soft and saggy. Fortunately medication kept him drowsy or sleeping most of the first two days.

Our greatest need was a rental house. The owner of the motel mentioned a summer cabin on the highway, about five hundred feet from where we were staying. Normally the homeowner didn't rent it out, but because he knew Tom through Scouting, he was willing to rent the house to us for two or three months. We could move in the following weekend. The best part was it was fully furnished.

Everyday while at the motel, I stood outside with Katy as she waited for the bus, helped Tom with his needs, loaded the dogs into the car and went to the ranch to build the fires for the day. And every day to get to the house, I had to use the pickax to clear the ice on the driveway. Sometimes while I swung the ax, I yelled out or cried from the frustration and exhaustion of having so many responsibilities. At other times, I gave thanks for people's help in finding an alternate place to live, Katy's joy in being closer to her friends, and our decision earlier in the year to put the ranch on the market. Without Tom's help, I wouldn't be able to manage. The damage to his knee was permanent.

Receiving the keys to the rental house was like being given the keys to the kingdom. There was a master bedroom on the first floor with a firm bed for Tom. It was next to the bathroom, convenient to the kitchen and had easy access to the living room couch. The school bus stop was at our front door and Katy was excited because she could sleep later in the morning. We were in heaven!

Two days after moving into the house, I woke up with my eyes swollen shut and my body covered with large red welts. I drove myself to the doctor looking through tiny slits struggling against the pain of the sunlight. The combination of chemicals in the house from brand new carpet and the stress of the previous week had led to a case of hives.

Injected with a large dose of antihistamine and more medicine in hand, I drove back to the house and slept. For the next two months when I left the house, the hives cleared a little. When I went back in, they became worse.

Tom and I were quite the pair with our ailments and drugs. But Katy enjoyed the time, spending long hours with friends who got off the bus with her after school to play at our house. I drove them the short distance to their homes when it got late.

For Katy, the Double K was momentarily forgotten, but I thought I could continue having guests while Tom was recovering. In the first month that proved impossible. He couldn't move easily and the medication made him unsteady both physically and emotionally. I canceled several groups. Although we missed the income, it was too exhausting running back and forth.

One of the few amusements during this time was Tom's run-down on the "soaps" and game shows he gave me when I came back. to the house each day. He had never stayed at home during his working career and at first was delighted to watch "The Price is Right," and "Family Feud." As a joke he learned the names of some of the characters on "General Hospital" and teased me about how he could get used to staying home.

But he was impatient with the healing process and the length of recovery. As he began physical therapy and slowly regained the use of his leg, his temperament improved. With a big brace stabilizing his leg, I was able to take him to work for part of each day after four weeks. The change of scenery, and a place to go with work to do, was the best therapy of all.

The weather warmed, daylight lengthened and the sound of the Naches River, which ran right beside the rental house, soothed our weary spirits. With the kitchen windows open, I could hear the water moving over rocks making its swift turn just before the house. Even though the air had a little chill in the evenings, eating outside "picnic style" was Katy's favorite activity. When Tom and I got too cold to stay out any longer, the dogs stayed with Katy as willing participants. As long as she fed them they were more than happy to oblige.

Two months after the accident, Tom was again able to drive himself to work. We began moving our things out of the rental and back up to the ranch. We were looking forward to returning to the lodge, a place that was truly our own even if not permanent.

Chapter Forty-Two

CO-EXISTING

It took an hour and a half one way each time I drove to Yakima for supplies, for lessons for Katy or to teach my own music students at the college. But the reward was in the wildlife I saw along the road. Elk, deer, fox and bobcats, and smaller animals like raccoons and skunks, appeared beside the road bringing a sense of awe and delight to the sometimes-lonely trip. Twice I spotted a cougar scaling the rocky ledge. At dusk, the deer would be at the roadside ready to dash across, hopping like kangaroos in chaos. At night, the elk, a calmer species, stood regally in the grassy space between the forest and the road and the car's headlights became a spotlight for the bull elk's magnificent antlers pointing skyward. Smaller animals appeared during the day heading for cover or searching for food. I often stopped to watch their progress as they paused, looked around, and then scurried across the pavement knowing the hard surface was not part of the natural forest floor. Some of the less fortunate animals never made it to the other side.

Seeing dead animals on the road made me queasy and sad. The queasiness was no doubt involved in the idea of the randomness of death: having no say in the place, time, or manner in which one's life is taken. Living in the midst of the wilderness I came to love the wild creatures, their antics and the surprises they brought to me. It made me sad to see one of them lying twisted and bloodied, thrown aside by a metal monster with a horsepower engine, their beauty and particular animal nature wasted and forgotten.

I felt compelled to pray for these animals. I wondered where the essence, the spirit, of the creature had gone when death abruptly ended its life on the lonely stretch of road from the highway to our drive. In some way I hoped my prayer would honor the dignity of the animal, even in its death. I prayed for a final resting place for their spirits.

I hit a bobcat once. I was on my way back to the Double K after Tom's Super Bowl Sunday accident. As I drove further from the reflective lights of the city, the darkness closed in on all sides. I was scared to drive on the wintry roads late at night, but I needed to get the dogs to take them back to town. The fire in the coal furnace had to be built up to stay burning in case of colder weather and the faucets left dripping so the system wouldn't freeze and crack the pipes.

I traveled as fast as I could on the snow-packed road occasionally hitting an icy patch and slowing until the road looked clear again. My body was running on the energy of fear and anxiety, and my mind skipped from one thought to another working out what had to be done the next day to meet my family's needs. I was almost at the turn-off for Goose Prairie when a bobcat raced out from the trees at the side of the road. Pumping my brakes on the icy pavement, I swerved to avoid the cat that looked stunned and scared in the headlights. Even with braking, the car moved ahead and I heard the dreaded thud.

I finally got the car stopped and ran back to where I had hit the bobcat. I looked all around on the pavement and checked the brush alongside the road. The beam from my flashlight revealed nothing in the trees on either side of the road. There was no sign of the animal. I stood in the cold, shivering and over-come with hopelessness. There was nothing to do but go on to

Goose Prairie. I got in the car and drove, sobbing all the way to the lodge.

Driving up the lane, I parked the car in the field below the lodge and hiked through the wet, heavy snow to get to the building. I stoked the furnace and closed the damper as much as I could so that the fire would burn slowly. After checking all the faucets and doors and windows, I loaded the dogs into the car for the journey back to the motel in Yakima. I slowed to search the roadway one last time on the way back to town, but it was fruitless.

Every time I passed that spot, I thought about the bobcat. Had I wounded him? Had he managed to drag himself into the woods and died there? Maybe I had hit the cat in a way that made a horrible sound but hadn't injured him.

It was a blessing to both of us that I didn't find the bobcat that night. I'm not sure what I would have done if I had. The mercy of Mother Nature was with me. I had to get back to tend to my own family and knew nothing about caring for injured wildlife. Maybe the bobcat was given the gift of a longer life in spite of its injury. If not, I hope his spirit found peace somewhere in the deep snow and darkness of that lonely January night.

A huge dead tree stood behind the lodge on forest service land. We weren't allowed to cut it down even though it would soon fall. Each day I watched a Pileated Woodpecker working on getting the ants out of it. His head whipped back and forth as his beak drove into the bark like a miniature jackhammer on a highway job. The sound got more intense as his head moved faster and faster and the pile of sawdust grew larger at the base of the tree. As suddenly as it started, it stopped. Once again began the rap-rap-rapping on the tree's trunk. Mealtimes for this bird were frequent, noisy and, hopefully, satisfying.

Another bird had identical frequency and noise but not the same satisfaction. One rainy spring morning I heard a frightening sound. At first I could not identify the noise's origin but soon realized it was coming from the second floor or attic. I climbed the stairs, listening and at the top of the stairs, determined that the sound was in the attic.

As I stepped onto the attic floor the noise stopped. I started back down. Before I reached the bottom the clamor started once more. I moved quickly hoping to catch the culprit in the act. The noise continued but I didn't see anything in the attic. I went outside and looked up.

Sitting on the peak of the roof was a woodpecker. Not a Pileated one, but a small Hairy Woodpecker. He was busy hammering hard on the metal. Again and again his little head speedily poked at the roof trying to get whatever he sensed was in there. I threw some small rocks up on the edge of the metal and, startled by the noise, the bird flew away.

A few minutes later the sound began again. I went out, threw more rocks and again he flew away. I stayed outside to see if he would return immediately. He didn't. No, the little guy waited until I was back in the house.

I gave up chasing him away and for the next half-hour we co-existed. He returned several days at different times, then disappeared for good. Cute guy. What he didn't have in brains he certainly had in perseverance.

At Thanksgiving the following year a raccoon came to visit and he had brains. In the woodshed, outside the kitchen door and across the dirt drive, were stacks of wood and a large, square, metal cold box. The box provided a place for storing pies, leftovers, and cheeses, to be used in the near future. They stayed cold, didn't take up room in the refrigerator, and were safe from animals' prying paws.

Our guests had finished dinner. After cleaning up the table and dishes, I went to get the pies from the shed. The lights were on. Just from habit, I looked around, making sure that there were no animals present. I opened the door of the cold box, took out four pies, set two of them on the wood stack and closed the door. I could only carry three pies at once so I left one of them there and quickly went to the house with the others.

I set them down on the kitchen counter and went out the back door to get the other pie. Entering the shed, I was startled to see a raccoon sitting on the wood stack holding the pie in his lap, using his other paw to scoop up the pumpkin and piecrust. The light in the shed provided a spotlight for him and my presence didn't bother him at all. With his little bandit-like mask and bushy, banded tail, he looked like a small Zorro who had completed his task and was now enjoying the reward.

Walking past him into the shed, I sat on the wood stack opposite the raccoon and watched him as he ate. He didn't seem to be in a hurry but he didn't leave a lot of time between bites either. He looked at each handful and then stuffed it in his mouth, licking between and around his fingers after each bite. As he did all this he occasionally looked over at me and then dug into the pan once again.

When the pie pan was almost empty, he put it up to his face and tried to get every last crumb from the bottom and sides. He laid the pan on the woodpile exactly where it had been, climbed down the logs and ambled out of the shed into the darkness. I sat there to savor the last few moments before returning to the house to enjoy the pies that were left.

Chapter Forty-Three

MY KIND OF WOMAN

S pring in Goose Prairie was as beautiful as winter was harsh. The dogs delighted in their freedom to roam without leashes. Katy awaited the opening of the Goose Prairie Inn and visited all the neighbors in anticipation. Tom and I, thankful at the progress he was making, mulled over an offer to purchase the ranch from two women in Seattle.

They had made this offer, which was way under our asking price, in the fall. Included were fifteen pages of small, printed material in legal language with many exceptions to the main offer. The agreement, written by a lawyer in Seattle, outlined at least five different exit clauses for the buyer with no penalties to them and unlimited liability to us. Through our agent we had countered each of their offers with what we thought was a reasonable agreement. But each time they countered back, the document contained a greater number of exceptions.

More importantly, I didn't like the women. Their attitude was one of doing us a favor by being interested in our property. They had stayed at the Double K with Kay and Isabelle, which they believed gave them some inside knowledge about the property. They wanted to use the ranch as an extension of their "kitsch" business in Seattle. I wasn't sure how they were going to do that, but it made my stomach queasy whenever it was mentioned.

The offer cooled for a while during Tom's accident and recovery, but with the weather improving and access to the ranch increasing each day, the women were urging us toward a decision. We wanted to move before the next school year began, but we were also unwilling to take a loss on the property or saddle ourselves with unreasonable demands in order to move.

My friend Ilene, who came to visit for a day, had an idea, which came from her Catholic friends.

"Kathleen," she said, "you need to buy a statue of St. Joseph and plant him on your property. If you're selling a property you plant him upside down and facing outwards. If you want a property, you have to plant St. Joseph upside down and facing *toward* the property. It works, according to my friends. You'll get what you want!"

Me, a minister, planting Catholic statuary on my property? The next few weeks found me searching for a small St. Joseph in the religious shops in Yakima. I explained to the shop owners why I wanted St. Joe, hoping they would verify the success of burying a saint in the dirt. Finally, at a Catholic store in Seattle, I located a six-inch statue of the venerable one and carried him home.

"You're going to do what?" Tom stared at me in disbelief.

"I'm going to plant the saint on the front corner of the property down by the creek. Are you going to help or not?"

"Sure," he said. "I wouldn't miss this for the world. I'll get the shovel."

We went down the drive. On the corner of the lot closest to the road Tom dug a hole. I shoved St. Joseph in head first, face pointed outward. Tom threw the dirt back on top until the little feet were no longer visible. He tapped the top of the mound with his foot.

"Here's hoping the dogs don't dig him up before the sale goes through."

"Hey," I said, "it's worth a shot. Maybe it will work. But I think we have to really believe."

He leaned on the shovel and laughed. "You believe. I dug the hole."

"Stop laughing. If it works, the lodge will be sold in no time."

In the days that followed we forgot about St. Joseph. Some of the winter parties had rescheduled, and there were several large groups holding their own retreats and meetings in the lodge. A number of women from Yakima came to the ranch on an April weekend to enjoy each other's company and the outdoors. The sky was spectacular. The sun shone brightly and daffodils were beginning to show through the melting snow. The women spent most of their time walking, talking, drinking coffee, and enjoying the ambience of the great room and the fire in the evenings. On Saturday night I joined the women as they sat around the living room.

"I hear you're selling the ranch," said Kay, one of the women in the group. "Doesn't it break your heart?"

"We have to sell. Tom can't help any more. But we had already decided last fall to put it on the market. Katy's going into middle school and wants to participate in more activities. And truthfully, I'm tired. To live here would be work enough. To live here and have guests...." I sat down at the table with her.

"We have a big family house outside of Spokane," she told me, "but it's quite a ways away and we don't get there very often -- occasionally for family get-togethers. But that's all."

She told me more about her family and the house as well as the celebrations they had there. The women probably brought all kinds of potluck dishes to share, I thought, and everyone sat around a big table all talking at once. I imagined the children being put to bed, then secretly gathering to read stories by flashlight, giggling and tiptoeing here and there thinking their parents were ignorant of the activity.

"It sounds perfect. Do you miss spending time there?"

"I miss having the family together in one place. All the children and the grandchildren. Room for everyone."

She looked outside, then around the room, seemingly from a distant place in her mind.

"I like this place. It has a great feel about it. Maybe <u>our</u> family should buy it."

What? After twenty-four hours she thought she might like to buy it? This was my kind of woman.

"I'll bring Dennis up to see what he thinks. What's the asking price?"

I told her and mentioned the land was already subdivided into parcels. The lodge and cottage sat on the biggest piece, two-and-a-half acres, and the rest we were offering as one-acre parcels. We wanted to sell the property to one buyer, but would be willing to divide it if necessary.

Prospective buyers had visited over the fall and spring, but most of them had heady dreams and very little money. Those with money, after contemplation about the amount of work involved in operating a ranch in the middle of the wilderness, chose not to make a serious offer. As I spoke to this woman, I tried not to get my hopes up.

The rest is a pleasant blur. Dennis and Kay visited the ranch, asked lots of questions, looked in every nook and cranny, upstairs and down, and made an offer. They wanted the house and the acreage around it, but not the other lots. The only stipulation was that a covenant be drawn up for the other properties so that no mobile homes could be placed there.

Oh, blessed St. Joseph, my kind of saint! On May 11, 1995, we signed a contract and a week later, received a check. The sale was final. We had three weeks to pack our belongings and move to Yakima.

Chapter Forty-Four

A BLAZING SURPRISE

E very night after dinner, Tom, Katy and I packed and played games – twenty minutes of packing and twenty minutes of gin rummy or a board game, then back to packing. About nine o'clock we were ready for much-needed sleep. On Thursday, May 25, Tom and Katy headed off to bed. This time of night, was dark, quiet, and still. I savored the feeling of contentment.

As I packed small utensils in the kitchen, read the newspaper, and wandered around looking at the house with admiration, I remembered the past five years and all the changes to our lives. I could hear Tom snoring up in the loft and Katy, who had chosen to spend the night in a bedroom upstairs in the lodge rather than in the loft, had fallen asleep as soon as I tucked her in.

I stood at the counter under the single gaslight reading the paper bulging with Memorial Day advertisements. Four unusually loud popping noises came from outside. I walked to the dining room window thinking it the beginning of an early holiday celebration. It was dark. Only the reflection of the light from the apartment shone outside. As I turned from the window, I heard a few more popping noises. I swung around quickly to catch the culprit. The ground outside was brightly illuminated like a yellow spotlight. Leaping flames were shooting out of the generator house window, huge tongues licking at the bushes outside.

"Tom! Get up! There's a fire. The generator house is on fire!"

"What?" he called from the loft.

"A fire!" I yelled. "The generator house is on fire!"

I went to the bottom of the lodge steps and called Katy.

"Katy, get up and come to the steps."

I ran back down to the apartment and grabbed the radio phone. Tom came down the loft ladder slowly because of his injured knee. Grabbing a small fire extinguisher we kept by the back door, he went outside in his pajamas. I knew the extinguisher wasn't enough, but he had to see the fire for himself. He came back in immediately and got into his clothes while I ran to get Katy. As she came down the lodge steps, she asked what was going on.

"Take these clothes and get dressed. Grab the dogs and get in the car. No questions, just do it!"

"Okay, Mama." Terror shone in her eyes, but the dear girl obeyed as if her life depended on it. She ran back up the steps never looking back.

By now the whole inside of the house was illuminated by the intensity of the flames' light. I dialed "911" on the radio phone and hoped it would work immediately. The signal got through but the reception was fuzzy. I tried to remain calm as I gave information to the Forest Service dispatcher in Wenatchee.

"I'm calling from Goose Prairie. There's a fire here bordering the wilderness area. We have thousand-gallon tanks of fuel involved." Stay calm, I thought. Stay calm.

"Please hang up and call from a different phone," she said. "Please call from a phone other than a cell phone. I can't understand you."

"Don't hang up!" I knew my voice was rising. "I'm on a radio phone in Goose Prairie. I don't have another phone."

"Please go to another phone. Your call isn't clear."
Wasn't she listening?

"I don't have another phone. The closest phone is sixteen miles away," I shouted. "Don't you understand? My house is going to burn down, the William O. Douglas Wilderness area is going to be on fire and I have to get my family to safety. Do you understand?"

"Just a minute." I could hear voices in the background. She came back on the line. "Ma'am?"

"I'm here, please help us!"

"What is the address?" She had me repeat it several times, but she was listening to me now.

"We're calling the Nile Fire Department and the Forest Service." The fire department was forty-five minutes away, but at least they were coming.

"Thank you so much," I yelled into the phone and hung up.

Down in the apartment Tom shouted into the CB radio trying to alert our neighbors.

"Please, someone, come in. We have a massive fire. The garage with the fuels and the generators is on fire! Someone, please, respond! Please!"

Katy scurried down the steps and called the dogs who came immediately. Even they sensed the urgency of the moment. She grabbed Bear's collar and headed out the back door. Samantha followed close behind. She got the dogs into the car and climbed in after them. I drove down to the meadow on the other side of the creek and left Katy and the dogs in the car.

"Don't get out of the car, Katy. Stay here where I know I can find you quickly."

"I'm scared, Mama." She wrapped her arms around Samantha's neck.

"I am too, honey."

"Is the house going to burn down?"

"I don't know, Katy. I hope not. We've got to be brave. Cuddle with the dogs and think good thoughts. I have to get clothes from the house and then I'll be right back. Remember, don't get out of the car."

"I won't. I promise."

She wedged herself between the two dogs in the back of the station wagon, an arm around each dog's neck. I shut the back of the car and headed up the hill to the house.

The loud explosions were unnerving. I felt scared as I entered the house. I moved quickly from room to room gathering what was most necessary for our day-to-day survival in the next few weeks. It was only a matter of time before the whole house became engulfed in flames and I prayed that I would be able to gather clothes, shoes, and a few valuables before that happened. I looked out the living room window as I searched through the desk drawers. The flames were now twenty-five feet above the tops of the trees. The explosions from the fuels occurred with greater frequency and intensity. How soon until the hundreds of gallons of gasoline and diesel exploded and spread the fire to the propane tanks?

Tom and I left the house with two black plastic bags stuffed with our valuables and walked quickly down the hill. Katy was still huddled in the back of the car with the two dogs. She was crying but tried to hide it. I grabbed her from the back and hugged her. Tom joined us and we huddled together trying to reassure each other.

Dick and Melva, two of our friends from the Prairie, came up the drive and offered to take Katy back to their house. I lifted a shivering, frightened girl out of the car and put her into Melva's arms. Katy wanted me to come with her, but I needed to stay with Tom until fire crews arrived. Sitting down on the edge of the car seat, I felt my heart beating irregularly and far too fast as they drove away. I breathed deeply, willing my heart to slow down.

When I felt better, Tom and I walked across the field, stood on the far side of the creek and looked up the hill. The fire illuminated everything within five hundred feet. The reflections of the flames in the large picture windows made it difficult for us to determine whether or not the house was on fire. As we stood watching, I became very calm and experienced a pervasive peace. There was nothing more we could do except wait for help to arrive. We had our child, our dogs and our lives. No matter what the outcome of this night, we would start over.

Two other friends from the Prairie arrived to see what they could do for us. Webb had been a firefighter in Tacoma. He and Tom walked up to the fire. Webb's wife, Sonda, and I waited for them to return, and when they didn't, we walked up the hill to see what was happening. The sky was still flooded with light from the flames but the explosions were not as loud or as often. Tom and Webb sat by the woodshed. Webb pointed things out in the burning structure down the hill to Tom.

"Webb thinks the fire won't spread and the house will be okay." Tom sounded hopeful. "He says he doesn't think the trees will sustain much damage either."

"The house will be fine," Webb said. "There's no wind. It will be okay as long as the tanks don't explode."

After sitting in silence for some time, we heard the sirens of the trucks in the distance, then honking and loud shouting at the end of the driveway. The fire trucks arrived two or three minutes later. Men jumped off the trucks and began to assess the situation. The supervisor asked Tom about the tanks and the materials that were in the garage and generator house. Firefighters worked to cool the ground around the mouths of the tanks so that they posed less of a threat to the remaining buildings. Every fifteen minutes or so, the tank truck went to the river to get water. Our generators, which had been used to bring water to the house, were now burned beyond recognition. Large amounts of burning metal created intense heat, but the fire itself seemed to be less powerful.

My body relaxed. Others were now in control. I felt shaky and my legs were beginning to tremble when I sat down. After telling Tom I was leaving, I walked down to the field and got in my car. Tom and Webb could stay and the firefighters could do their work. My daughter needed me and I needed to hold a small, scared girl.

I drove down the road. Summer neighbors and visitors from the campgrounds were everywhere. It was a terrifying night for them as well. A fire raging out of control could destroy their properties along with the forest.

Dick and Melva's house had become a community communications center. Our closest friends were gathered comforting Katy. In spite of her fear, she was enjoying being the center of attention. She jumped into my arms as I sat down with our prairie friends. We talked for a while, each person sharing his or her impression of the fire's impact. It all seemed surreal and far away to me as I tried to pay attention to what was being said.

Katy was becoming very heavy in my arms. I excused myself from the conversation as fatigue crept over me. We undressed quickly, put on the t-shirts I had grabbed from the house, and got into the beds Melva had prepared. Katy fell into a troubled sleep almost immediately. I lay awake trying to make sense of the evening's events.

The next morning I woke about five and got dressed. My clothes smelled like smoke. Dick had the coffee going in the kitchen. I grabbed a cup, saw that Katy was still asleep, and left to go see the remains of the fire in daylight. As I walked up the hill I smelled the watered down wood and metal – the distinctive smell of a fire scene. A fire truck from the Bureau of Land Management (BLM) was parked in the driveway. Tom was coming out of the house with a flask of coffee for the men sitting around the woodshed.

I rounded the corner of the house and saw the charred timbers that had formed the structure of the generator house. The stately fir trees, which circled the building, were burned, but only on the side facing the destroyed structure. The table saw, wood splitter and snow blower were burnt sculptures of their former selves dipping here and there like the framework of miniature roller coasters. All were the same burnt gray-black color. Shiny places on the burned metal, where aluminum from the roof had melted and fallen like specks of gold leaf, made it look like modernistic work of art.

The propane canisters whose tops had blown off in the intense heat were strewn about the ground and chunks of burned materials two inches deep covered the whole area. Nails, no longer any good, were scattered about the ground and the copper wire, which had hung in a back corner of the garage, was curled there still.

Tom was exhausted from staying up all night. Since the BLM people had to stay the rest of the morning to be sure the danger was over, there wouldn't be any sleep for him. I drove to town, called the new owners, and told them about the fire. They were gracious, asking first if we were okay and then offering help if we needed it. Their understanding was a blessing.

That evening Katy and I stayed at the neighbor's house again, while Tom slept in the lodge. Without the generators, we had no water or power to the building but the preparation for moving had to go on in spite of that. It was several days before Katy could make herself go back to the house to stay and weeks before she slept alone.

I am amazed how calmly and logically I moved about the house once I discovered the fire. I had the presence of mind to grab our business and family checkbooks, irreplaceable documents, and the financial reports of the ranch all of which contained the best inventory of our business and personal items. It is good to know how well one can respond in emergencies, to automatically do what must be done – while emotions shut down against the full impact of the momentous event.

Chapter Forty-Five

REFLECTION ON THE SHORELINE

How is it possible to want something so much and then let it go? This question tugged as I wandered along the shoreline of Bumping Lake. The air was chilly for a June day. A light breeze danced last fall's leaves around my feet like tiny dervishes under the spell of Mother Earth. Delicate puffs of cloud floated by in the Mediterranean blue sky and their shadows on the water seemed like boats passing swiftly by the shore.

The dogs had run ahead, and Sam, with her front feet in the lake, turned to look at me for permission to take a swim.

"Go for it, Sammy," I yelled. She leaped joyfully toward the deeper water and quickly scrambled back onto the beach. She shook herself briskly and ran along the sand to Bear, who was sniffing and pawing near a stand of trees.

I stopped, breathed deeply and closed my eyes, wanting to experience the feeling of this place, the calm extravagance of its beauty pouring over me like rich oil. I opened my eyes and turned my head slowly, gathering in the landscape of mountains, pines, and the lake's reflection of both. I would never have this again in this way. How much I would have liked time to stand still.

Memories came and went like children playing hide and seek among the trees. The ambiguity of our mountain existence provided a backdrop to these recollections. The remoteness of our ranch and the solitude it had given us played against the inability of repair people to get to the ranch to work and our lack of means to pay for necessary repairs. We took pleasure in seeing elk, deer, bobcats, cougar, bear and silver fox in their natural habitat on a regular basis, but residing with them also meant living with mice, carpenter ants, squirrels, muskrats and bats in our house.

I thought about the joy of Katy's life in Goose Prairie. Adults doted on her, the expressive nature of the forest in each season surrounded her, and she explored the forest on her own without fear or restraint. It seemed like a child's paradise. But the lack of friends who lived nearby and the distance to school each day accompanied by her exhaustion dampened the joy.

Would I have begged and made deals with the devil if I had known the challenges, anxiety and physical pain buying the ranch would bring? I don't know. Thoreau, in his "Journal, 1851" said, "A ticket to heaven must include tickets to limbo, purgatory and hell". I certainly bought several tickets to each of those places without knowing it when Tom and I purchased the Double K!

I was such a mountain novice and seemingly so different than Kay and Isabelle. The mountains permeated everything they said and did whether it was a campaign to set aside land as wilderness area or taking guests to the lakes high in the Cascades. They spent their free time riding into uncharted territory. They found new places to explore and eventually shared them with their guests. Isabelle once wrote in "Dude Rancher" magazine that, on a ride into the mountains, "We had no idea where we were. We camped that night by an unknown stream in a forgotten meadow. We were lost and didn't care." They didn't mind spending the night in a leaky tent, or being soaked by a surprise snowstorm in late September.

I needed a place where, as Hans Kung said in his memoir "the self is taken up into the whole but where one's self is not lost." Wide mountain vistas, the clouds moving in quickly from the far range, the sunset filling the sky with red then gold and the moon throwing a veil of gossamer white over the forest were the things that moved me to explore the uncharted territory of my own life, making me feel as if I were a part of something much greater than I knew. I had hoped to bring others to the ranch to do that same kind of exploration. Perhaps there were a few who felt the Double K was a place where they could journey in safety.

Surrounded by a natural world of this magnitude and power, I also became fully aware of my mortality. I could not control the amount of snow, the abundance or lack of water, the "when" and "if" of a fast moving mountain storm, the wildlife inhabiting our acreage, or trees, which stretched to catch a glimpse of sunlight in the midst of the forest. I was merely human and sometimes barely in control of myself. What a mystery - to be grounded by the very nature that allowed me to be "taken up into the whole."

What I wanted and what I got were often two different things. I thought I was going to be the lady of the manor, working hard, but adored by the public who came to the Double K for renewal and rest. I would die there surrounded by all that I loved. What I got was a lot of never-ending hard work, great friends, stories, gifts of time and love from people I had never met before they came to the ranch, and five astonishing years.

Not only did the ranch give me things I never imagined, but it also tested my character. How tough was I? How persistent in my ability to subdue hardship and how much personal fortitude could I muster when faced with failure at so many turns in the road? In its wisdom, the universe gave me what I needed and I discovered I was a much stronger person than I ever believed.

Loud barking interrupted my thoughts. Bear was busy jumping at the base of a tree and Samantha ran around acting like she knew what the problem was. The dogs wandered through the brush as if they were in hot pursuit, ran back to the water's edge, and finally sat down beside me. I knew they were anxious to run but they waited patiently for me to get up.

"Okay, you sweet girls, we'll be on our way." Samantha and Bear ran ahead oblivious to the changes facing us all. We were packed, and the truck was arriving tomorrow. I brushed the sand off my pants, gave the lake one last look, and walked toward the road.